Financial Independence

Alex Thompson

Published by Side Hustle Success, 2023.

AF725106

While every precaution has been taken in the preparation of this book, the publisher assumes no responsibility for errors or omissions, or for damages resulting from the use of the information contained herein.

FINANCIAL INDEPENDENCE

First edition. August 29, 2023.

Copyright © 2023 Alex Thompson.

ISBN: 979-8223546795

Written by Alex Thompson.

Dedication

To those who dare to dream, who embark on journeys of self-discovery, and who strive for financial independence—may your path be illuminated with knowledge, guided by determination, and enriched with the joy of progress.

Author's Note:

As you turn the last page of "Financial Independence," I want to express my sincere gratitude for joining me on this journey. Your dedication to improving your financial well-being is inspiring, and I hope this book has provided valuable insights and strategies to guide you toward your goals.

If you found this book helpful in your pursuit of financial independence, I kindly invite you to consider sharing your thoughts with others. Your honest review can serve as a guiding light for those who are seeking similar empowerment and guidance. Your feedback helps build a community of individuals working toward a shared vision of financial freedom.

Thank you for your time, your dedication, and your commitment to your own financial journey. Here's to your continued success and fulfillment.

Warm regards,

Alex Thompson

Defining Financial Independence

Financial independence represents a pivotal concept in personal finance, epitomizing a state of fiscal self-reliance that extends beyond traditional employment norms. It encapsulates the dynamic stage where an individual's accumulated wealth, investments, and passive income converge to not only maintain a preferred lifestyle but also to unlock the potential for pursuing aspirations devoid of financial constraints.

At its essence, financial independence empowers individuals to navigate life's crossroads guided by personal values rather than financial obligations. It's a journey distinguished from conventional retirement, as it doesn't mandate an absolute cessation of work, but rather confers the autonomy to shape work on one's own terms.

Defining financial independence involves acknowledging its intricate components:

Savings and Investments: The bedrock of financial independence lies in diligent savings and astute investments. By consistently allocating a portion of income to various investment vehicles such as stocks, bonds, real estate, and retirement accounts, individuals nurture the growth of their financial arsenal.

Passive Income Streams: A linchpin of financial independence is the cultivation of passive income sources. These streams, generated from investments or ventures requiring minimal day-to-day involvement, furnish a steady influx of funds even when active work diminishes.

Expense Prudence: A cardinal principle in the pursuit of financial independence is prudent expense management. Embracing frugality, monitoring expenditures, and making discerning spending choices converge to optimize finances and curtail the funding needed to uphold desired standards of living.

Debt Management: Strategically managing and reducing debt represents a critical stride towards financial independence. Conquering high-interest debts averts the depletion of wealth-building endeavors, hastening the expedition towards fiscal liberation.

Long-Term Strategy: A comprehensive financial plan underscores the foundation of financial independence. This roadmap delineates short and long-term financial objectives, charts the trajectory for their attainment, and strategizes responses to unanticipated financial curves.

The Path to Financial Independence

Embarking on the journey to financial independence entails navigating a personalized path influenced by variables like income, current financial obligations, and investment preferences. Though the expedition is uniquely shaped, fundamental steps form the scaffolding for this transformative voyage:

Self-Assessment: The journey commences with an unvarnished evaluation of present financial circumstances. Grasping the starting point provides the compass for charting the course ahead.

Goal Setting: Concrete short and long-term financial objectives must be outlined. From eradicating debts to attaining specific investment milestones, these goals underpin the expedition to financial autonomy.

Budget Crafting: Forging a well-defined budget that mirrors priorities is pivotal. Pinpointing domains where expenses can be streamlined empowers heightened savings and augmented investment contributions.

Building Reserves: Erecting an emergency fund, equivalent to several months' worth of expenses, acts as a financial buffer against unexpected fiscal ripples.

Strategic Investing: Scrutinizing investment avenues aligned with personal risk tolerance and objectives is a cornerstone. Diversification mitigates risk and augments potential returns.

Cultivating Passive Income: Delving into channels that generate passive income, such as dividend-bearing stocks or real estate ventures, forges a robust fortress of fiscal stability.

Progress Tracking: A consistent vigil over financial advancement, accompanied by recalibrations as needed, safeguards the feasibility and realism of objectives.

In essence, to define financial independence is to elucidate a realm wherein individuals construct a robust financial base that not only sustains their desired lifestyle but also emancipates them from the straitjacket of financial reliance. This journey is a symphony of calculated steps, resonating with prudence, strategic thinking, and the unwavering commitment to aligning financial choices with future aspirations.

Why Financial Independence Matters

The significance of financial independence reverberates through myriad aspects of an individual's life, touching upon not only economic matters but also emotional well-being, personal freedom, and the capacity to pursue aspirations unburdened by financial constraints. Its relevance is far-reaching, bestowing a multitude of advantages that span beyond the realm of money:

Freedom of Choice: Financial independence is synonymous with the freedom to make choices based on personal preferences rather than monetary obligations. It liberates individuals from being tethered to jobs solely for financial sustenance, enabling them to explore unconventional careers, philanthropic endeavors, or taking time off for personal pursuits.

Reduced Stress and Anxiety: The weight of financial uncertainty often contributes to stress and anxiety. Achieving financial independence alleviates this burden, fostering a sense of security and tranquility that emanates from the knowledge that one's financial needs are met.

Pursuit of Passions: Freed from the shackles of financial dependency, individuals can channel their energies toward passions and hobbies without fear of compromising their livelihood. This can lead to enhanced personal satisfaction and a more fulfilling life.

Improved Work-Life Balance: Financial independence facilitates the pursuit of a work-life equilibrium. Individuals can scale down work commitments, explore part-time roles, or even retire early to dedicate more time to family, leisure, and personal growth.

Generational Impact: Attaining financial independence has the potential to create a positive ripple effect for future generations. It enables parents to provide better education, support, and opportunities for their children, setting the stage for improved quality of life down the line.

Entrepreneurial Ventures: Financial independence affords individuals the latitude to explore entrepreneurial ventures without the fear of financial ruin.

This fosters innovation, creativity, and the potential to contribute to economic growth.

Philanthropy and Social Impact: Individuals who achieve financial independence are often better positioned to engage in philanthropy and social impact initiatives. They can contribute their time, expertise, and resources to causes they're passionate about, effecting positive change in their communities and beyond.

Mitigating Age-Related Concerns: Financial independence can be a powerful buffer against age-related concerns such as healthcare expenses and retirement. Having a robust financial cushion allows for more comprehensive planning and preparedness for the later stages of life.

Strengthened Relationships: Financial independence can enhance personal relationships by reducing financial conflicts and stressors within families and partnerships. Clearer financial security can promote open communication and mutual support.

Lifelong Learning and Growth: Financial independence can support a lifelong pursuit of learning and personal development. Individuals can invest in education, skills, and experiences that contribute to continuous growth and a more enriched life.

In summary, the importance of financial independence extends well beyond the realm of finances. It lays the groundwork for a life characterized by personal autonomy, reduced stress, and the freedom to explore passions and pursuits. Achieving financial independence can foster improved mental and emotional well-being, amplify the capacity to make meaningful contributions to society, and unlock a future marked by choice, empowerment, and a heightened quality of life.

The Difference Between Financial Independence and Retirement

Financial independence and retirement are often used interchangeably, yet they represent distinct stages in a person's financial journey. While they share certain similarities, such as the desire for freedom from financial constraints, they diverge in their focus, purpose, and implications:

Focus and Purpose:

- **Financial Independence:** The central focus of financial independence is achieving a state where an individual's financial resources, including savings, investments, and passive income, are substantial enough to cover their expenses and desired lifestyle. The purpose of financial independence is to gain the freedom to make choices based on personal values, passions, and aspirations, whether that involves continuing to work, pursuing entrepreneurship, or dedicating time to hobbies.
- **Retirement:** Retirement, on the other hand, is typically associated with the cessation of full-time employment. The purpose of retirement is to transition from the workforce into a period of leisure and relaxation, often in the later stages of life. Retirement involves withdrawing from the daily grind of work to enjoy the fruits of years of labor.

Timing:

- **Financial Independence:** Financial independence can be achieved at any age when an individual's passive income and accumulated wealth can sustain their chosen lifestyle. Some people attain financial independence in their 30s or 40s, while others may reach it later in life.
- **Retirement:** Retirement is generally associated with the later stages of one's career, typically occurring around traditional retirement age,

which is often between 60 and 70 years old, depending on the country and social norms.

Work and Lifestyle:

- **Financial Independence:** Achieving financial independence doesn't necessarily mean stopping work altogether. Individuals who are financially independent have the flexibility to choose work that aligns with their interests, passions, and goals, regardless of the compensation.
- **Retirement:** Retirement typically involves stepping away from full-time employment. While some retirees choose to pursue part-time work, consulting, or other low-stress activities, the primary focus is on relaxation, leisure, and spending time on personal interests.

Financial Considerations:

- **Financial Independence:** Achieving financial independence involves creating a portfolio of investments, passive income streams, and a sufficient emergency fund. The emphasis is on maintaining a balance between income and expenses to sustain the desired lifestyle.
- **Retirement:** Retirement planning includes factors like estimating post-retirement expenses, optimizing Social Security benefits (or equivalent programs), and making decisions about pension payouts. The goal is to ensure that retirees can maintain their desired standard of living without being reliant on active work income.

Mindset:

- **Financial Independence:** The mindset associated with financial independence is one of empowerment and choice. Individuals who achieve financial independence feel a sense of control over their financial destiny and have the liberty to pursue their passions and interests.

- **Retirement:** Retirement often comes with a shift in mindset from a focus on career goals and financial accumulation to relaxation and leisure. It can be a time to explore new hobbies, travel, and spend quality time with loved ones.

In essence, while financial independence and retirement both involve the pursuit of financial security and freedom, they differ in their timing, purpose, and the emphasis on work. Financial independence offers individuals the flexibility to craft a life based on their preferences, whether it involves continuing to work or not, while retirement marks a transition into a phase of life centered around leisure and relaxation. Both stages, however, are underpinned by the fundamental goal of attaining greater autonomy and a fulfilling life.

Common Misconceptions About Financial Independence

The journey to financial independence is accompanied by a myriad of misconceptions and misunderstandings that can hinder individuals from making informed decisions about their finances. Unraveling these misconceptions is crucial for fostering a clearer understanding of what financial independence truly entails:

Early Retirement is the Only Goal:

- **Misconception:** Many assume that financial independence revolves solely around retiring early. While early retirement is a popular goal, financial independence doesn't necessitate retiring at a young age. It's about having the choice to work on your own terms or pursue other interests.

High Income Guarantees Financial Independence:

- **Misconception:** Earning a high income is beneficial, but financial independence isn't solely determined by income. Managing expenses, saving consistently, and making prudent investments play equally significant roles.

It Requires Extraordinary Luck:

- **Misconception:** Some believe that achieving financial independence is reserved for the exceptionally fortunate. While external factors can influence the journey, diligent planning, consistent efforts, and informed financial choices are pivotal.

Financial Independence Means Extreme Frugality:

- **Misconception:** While frugality can accelerate the path to financial independence, it doesn't mandate a life of extreme deprivation. The focus should be on optimizing spending, aligning expenses with values, and making conscious choices.

Debt is Always Detrimental:

- **Misconception:** While high-interest debt can impede progress, not all debt is detrimental. Leveraging low-interest debt for investments, such as real estate, can be strategic if approached cautiously.

It Requires a Large Inheritance:

- **Misconception:** Relying solely on a potential inheritance is an uncertain strategy. Financial independence is best achieved through proactive planning, disciplined saving, and investment strategies.

Achieving It is Quick and Easy:

- **Misconception:** Achieving financial independence is a gradual process that demands patience and consistent effort. Quick fixes and shortcuts rarely lead to sustainable results.

Investments are Too Risky:

- **Misconception:** While investments carry risk, avoiding them entirely can hinder wealth growth. Educated investment choices, diversification, and risk management can mitigate potential downsides.

It's All About Sacrifice:

- **Misconception:** The pursuit of financial independence doesn't mandate an austere lifestyle devoid of enjoyment. Balancing prudent financial decisions with enjoying life's experiences is key.

Financial Advisors are Unnecessary:

- **Misconception:** While some choose a self-directed approach, financial advisors can offer valuable guidance tailored to individual circumstances, optimizing financial strategies and enhancing the likelihood of success.

It's Only for High Earners:

- **Misconception:** Financial independence is attainable by individuals with various income levels. It's more about optimizing income and expenses than sheer earnings.

It Guarantees Permanent Bliss:

- **Misconception:** Financial independence can provide freedom, but it doesn't exempt individuals from life's challenges. It's a tool that empowers better decision-making but doesn't eliminate all difficulties.

Investments Always Perform Well:

- **Misconception:** Investments can be volatile, and returns aren't guaranteed. Diversification and a long-term perspective are crucial for managing investment risks.

Retirement Accounts Are the Only Way:

- **Misconception:** While retirement accounts offer tax advantages, other investment options and passive income sources also contribute to financial independence.

Addressing these misconceptions is integral to fostering a realistic perspective on financial independence. It's a multifaceted journey that necessitates well-informed decisions, adaptability, and a commitment to aligning financial strategies with individual goals and values.

Case Studies: Real-Life Examples of Financial Independence Achievers

Real-life case studies of individuals who have successfully attained financial independence serve as inspiring and educational narratives. These stories highlight the diverse paths, challenges, and strategies that individuals employ to reach this milestone, shedding light on the possibilities within everyone's reach:

The Early Retiree: Mr. and Mrs. Smith

- **Background:** The Smiths, in their mid-40s, aimed for early retirement. They both worked in tech fields, saved aggressively, and invested in a mix of index funds and rental properties.
- **Strategy:** They maintained a frugal lifestyle, investing over 50% of their income. Rental income and dividends from investments covered their expenses.
- **Impact:** The Smiths retired at 45, enabling them to travel extensively and engage in philanthropy. Their story showcases the power of disciplined saving, prudent investing, and a focused goal.

The Entrepreneurial Couple: Alex and Lisa

- **Background:** Alex and Lisa started a successful online business. Their venture generated substantial income, but they sought more control over their time.
- **Strategy:** They diversified income streams through investments and real estate while continuing their business. This blend of active and passive income provided stability.
- **Impact:** By their late 30s, they achieved financial independence, giving them the freedom to explore new business ventures and spend quality time with their family.

The Middle Manager Turned Blogger: Sarah

- **Background:** Sarah, in her late 30s, worked as a middle manager but dreamt of more flexibility. She started a personal finance blog and monetized it over time.
- **Strategy:** Through affiliate marketing, sponsored content, and digital product sales, Sarah built a steady stream of passive income from her blog.
- **Impact:** Within a few years, her blog income exceeded her salary. She transitioned to part-time work, relishing in her newfound freedom and the ability to balance her passion with work.

The Real Estate Investor: Mark

- **Background:** Mark, an engineer in his early 40s, recognized the potential of real estate. He built a portfolio of rental properties over time.
- **Strategy:** Mark's rental income supplemented his salary, and he reinvested profits to acquire more properties. He focused on properties in growing markets.
- **Impact:** By his mid-50s, Mark achieved financial independence through rental income. His story showcases the value of leveraging real estate for passive income.

The Physician Pursuing Part-Time Work: Dr. Jackson

- **Background:** Dr. Jackson, a physician, desired a more balanced lifestyle without sacrificing income.
- **Strategy:** He negotiated a part-time schedule and supplemented his income with locum tenens work, consulting, and telemedicine.
- **Impact:** By his early 50s, Dr. Jackson achieved financial independence, enjoying a fulfilling medical career while having more time for leisure and travel.

The Hybrid Approach: Emily

- **Background:** Emily, in her 30s, wanted to pursue creative passions while ensuring financial stability.
- **Strategy:** She continued her day job but used her spare time to build a freelance writing career. Passive income from investments complemented her earnings.
- **Impact:** Emily achieved financial independence in her early 40s, balancing her creative pursuits with steady income and a secure future.

These case studies underscore that financial independence isn't a one-size-fits-all concept. It can be achieved through diverse routes, from disciplined saving, strategic investing, and entrepreneurial ventures to leveraging passive income sources and pursuing alternative career paths. Each story exemplifies the transformative power of aligning financial decisions with personal goals, passions, and values.

Setting Clear Financial Goals

Setting clear financial goals is the foundation upon which the journey to financial independence is built. Well-defined goals provide direction, motivation, and a roadmap for making informed decisions. Here's a comprehensive exploration of the process of setting clear financial goals:

The Importance of Clear Goals:

- Establishing precise financial goals is akin to plotting coordinates on a map. It gives individuals a clear destination and a sense of purpose, facilitating effective decision-making and resource allocation.

Types of Financial Goals:

- **Short-Term Goals:** These are objectives that can be achieved within a year or two, such as building an emergency fund, paying off a credit card debt, or saving for a vacation.
- **Medium-Term Goals:** These goals typically span three to five years and might include saving for a down payment on a house or funding higher education.
- **Long-Term Goals:** Goals with a horizon of five years or more, such as achieving financial independence, retiring comfortably, or leaving a legacy for future generations.

SMART Goal Framework:

- The SMART framework ensures goals are Specific, Measurable, Achievable, Relevant, and Time-Bound.
- **Specific:** Define goals with clarity and precision. For instance, instead of a vague goal like "Save for retirement," specify the target amount and timeline.
- **Measurable:** Goals should have quantifiable metrics. Being able to track progress and measure success provides motivation.

- **Achievable:** Goals should be realistic and attainable based on current circumstances. Stretch goals are encouraged, but they must also be within the realm of possibility.
- **Relevant:** Goals should align with individual values, aspirations, and the overall financial plan. They must be relevant to one's broader life goals.
- **Time-Bound:** Set a clear timeframe for achieving each goal. A deadline creates a sense of urgency and helps with planning.

Prioritizing Goals:

- Not all financial goals carry equal weight. Prioritize based on urgency and importance. Some goals might need to take precedence over others due to their time sensitivity or potential impact.

Quantifying Goals:

- Attach a specific monetary value to each goal. This figure provides a tangible target to work towards and helps in gauging progress.

Breaking Down Goals:

- Divide large goals into smaller, manageable steps. This makes the journey less overwhelming and creates a clear path forward.

Creating an Action Plan:

- Outline actionable steps required to achieve each goal. Identify resources needed, potential obstacles, and strategies for overcoming challenges.

Regular Review and Adjustments:

- Financial circumstances and priorities change over time. Regularly review goals and make adjustments as needed. Flexibility ensures alignment with evolving life situations.

Examples of Clear Financial Goals:

- Saving $10,000 in an emergency fund within the next 12 months.
- Paying off $5,000 in credit card debt within two years.
- Accumulating $50,000 for a down payment on a home in five years.
- Achieving $1 million in retirement savings by age 55.
- Generating $10,000 in passive income annually from dividend stocks within five years.

Setting clear financial goals is a dynamic process that requires introspection, planning, and ongoing commitment. These goals serve as the guiding stars, steering individuals towards financial independence while enabling them to embrace life's opportunities with confidence and purpose.

Budgeting for Financial Independence

Budgeting serves as a foundational tool on the journey to financial independence, providing a roadmap for allocating resources, controlling expenses, and maximizing savings. Here's an in-depth exploration of how to create an effective budget that aligns with the goal of achieving financial independence:

Understanding the Role of Budgeting:

- A budget is a financial blueprint that outlines income, expenses, and savings goals. It empowers individuals to make informed decisions about spending, saving, and investing.

Assessing Current Financial Situation:

- Begin by analyzing current income sources, including salary, bonuses, investments, and passive income. Evaluate expenses by categorizing them into fixed (mortgage, rent) and variable (groceries, entertainment) categories.

Defining Financial Independence Goals:

- Set specific financial independence goals. These goals will inform your budget and guide your allocation of resources.

Creating Categories:

- Divide expenses into categories like housing, transportation, groceries, entertainment, healthcare, and debt payments. This categorization allows for a comprehensive view of spending patterns.

Prioritizing Expenses:

- Differentiate between essential and discretionary expenses. Prioritize essential expenses while considering discretionary spending as areas where adjustments can be made.

Allocating Resources:

- Assign a specific percentage of your income to each category. This allocation should align with your financial independence goals.

Reducing Unnecessary Spending:

- Identify areas where spending can be reduced without compromising quality of life. Analyze subscriptions, dining out, and impulse purchases.

Emergency Fund and Savings:

- Allocate a portion of your budget to an emergency fund and various savings goals, including retirement, investments, and short-term objectives.

Tracking and Monitoring:

- Use tools like budgeting apps or spreadsheets to track expenses. Regularly review your spending to ensure you're staying within budgetary limits.

Adjustments and Flexibility:

- Be prepared to adjust your budget as circumstances change. Flexibility allows you to accommodate unexpected expenses or shifts in financial goals.

Debt Repayment Strategy:

- If you have debts, allocate funds for debt repayment. Use strategies like the debt snowball or debt avalanche method to systematically pay off debts.

Savings and Investments:

- Allocate a portion of your budget to savings and investments. Consider automating contributions to retirement accounts and investment portfolios.

Opportunities for Increasing Income:

- Look for opportunities to increase your income, such as taking on a side hustle or pursuing professional development to enhance earning potential.

Periodic Review:

- Regularly assess your budget to ensure it aligns with your financial goals and lifestyle changes. Review and adjust your budget annually or whenever significant changes occur.

Mindful Spending:

- Practice mindful spending by asking whether purchases align with your goals and values. This cultivates a conscious approach to financial decisions.

Celebrate Milestones:

- Acknowledge your progress by celebrating financial milestones reached through disciplined budgeting. It can motivate you to maintain your financial discipline.

Creating a budget that resonates with your financial independence goals requires dedication, discipline, and a clear understanding of your financial landscape. It's a dynamic process that empowers you to take control of your finances, allocate resources effectively, and inch closer to the freedom and autonomy that financial independence brings.

The Importance of Emergency Funds

An emergency fund is a financial safety net that serves as a critical component of the journey toward financial independence. This cushion of savings provides a buffer against unexpected expenses, job loss, or other financial emergencies. Here's an in-depth exploration of the importance of emergency funds in achieving financial independence:

Protection Against Unforeseen Events:

- Life is unpredictable, and unexpected events such as medical emergencies, car repairs, or sudden job loss can disrupt financial stability. An emergency fund provides a layer of protection to mitigate the impact of these unforeseen circumstances.

Preserving Financial Independence Goals:

- Without an emergency fund, individuals may be forced to tap into their investments or accrue high-interest debt to cover unexpected expenses. This can set back progress toward financial independence.

Avoiding Debt Accumulation:

- An emergency fund acts as a buffer, reducing the need to resort to credit cards or loans to cover emergencies. This prevents the accumulation of debt and the associated interest payments.

Minimizing Stress and Anxiety:

- Financial emergencies can cause stress and anxiety. Having an emergency fund in place offers peace of mind, knowing that you're prepared to handle unexpected financial challenges.

Maintaining Budgetary Discipline:

- An emergency fund allows you to stick to your budget even when unexpected expenses arise. It prevents the need to reallocate funds from other areas of your budget, ensuring that you stay on track toward financial goals.

Avoiding Impulsive Decisions:

- Financial emergencies can lead to hasty and irrational decisions. With an emergency fund, you have the time and resources to make well-thought-out choices instead of reacting impulsively.

Flexibility in Career Choices:

- An emergency fund can provide the freedom to make career changes, pursue entrepreneurial ventures, or take sabbaticals without the fear of financial insecurity.

Maintaining Investments:

- Having an emergency fund reduces the need to liquidate investments during market downturns or financial crises. This allows investments to recover and grow over time.

Tailored to Personal Circumstances:

- The size of an emergency fund varies based on factors like income, expenses, and individual risk tolerance. It's a customizable safety net that suits your specific situation.

Building Financial Confidence:

- An emergency fund instills a sense of financial confidence, knowing that you're prepared for whatever challenges life may throw your way.

Accelerating Financial Progress:

- By eliminating the need to divert funds from savings or investments for emergencies, an emergency fund helps you stay on track toward financial independence.

Gradual Growth and Regular Contributions:

- Start with a modest emergency fund and gradually build it over time. Regular contributions, even if small, add up to a substantial safety net.

Adapting to Life Changes:

- Life circumstances change, and an emergency fund provides the flexibility to adapt to new situations without compromising your financial goals.

Peace of Mind and Freedom:

- Ultimately, an emergency fund offers peace of mind and the freedom to focus on long-term financial objectives, bringing you closer to the attainment of financial independence.

In summary, an emergency fund isn't just a financial tool; it's a cornerstone of financial stability and independence. It empowers individuals to navigate the uncertainties of life without derailing their progress toward their goals. As you embark on your journey toward financial independence, prioritizing the establishment and growth of an emergency fund is a vital step toward securing your financial future.

Strategies for Paying Down Debt

Debt Snowball Method: The debt snowball method involves prioritizing debts from smallest to largest balance, regardless of interest rates. Make minimum payments on all debts, and allocate any extra funds to the smallest debt. Once the smallest debt is paid off, roll its payment into the next smallest debt, creating a "snowball" effect.

Debt Avalanche Method: The debt avalanche method focuses on tackling debts with the highest interest rates first. Make minimum payments on all debts and allocate extra funds to the debt with the highest interest rate. Once that debt is paid off, direct the freed-up payment toward the next highest interest debt.

Debt Consolidation: Consolidate multiple high-interest debts into a single loan or credit card with a lower interest rate. This simplifies payments and potentially reduces interest costs. However, it's crucial to ensure that the new terms are favorable and won't lead to more debt.

Balance Transfer: Transfer high-interest credit card balances to a card with a promotional 0% interest period. This can provide temporary relief from interest charges, allowing you to pay down the principal more quickly.

Personal Loan for Debt Payoff: Consider taking out a personal loan with a lower interest rate to pay off high-interest debts. This can lead to lower monthly payments and reduced interest costs.

Increase Income: Increase your income through part-time work, freelancing, or a side hustle. Allocating additional earnings toward debt payments accelerates the payoff process.

Cut Discretionary Expenses: Identify non-essential expenses that can be reduced or eliminated, such as dining out, entertainment, or subscription services. Redirect these funds toward debt repayment.

Negotiate Interest Rates: Contact creditors to negotiate lower interest rates. A reduced interest rate can lead to faster debt repayment and lower overall costs.

Use Windfalls: Apply unexpected windfalls, such as tax refunds or bonuses, directly to debt repayment. These lump-sum payments can make a significant dent in outstanding balances.

Avoid Incurring New Debt: While paying down existing debt, commit to avoiding new debt. Focus on changing spending habits and making conscious financial decisions.

Automate Payments: Set up automatic debt payments to ensure consistent contributions, minimizing the risk of missing payments.

Target One Debt at a Time: Focus on aggressively paying down one debt at a time while making minimum payments on other debts. This concentrated effort can lead to quicker progress.

Monitor Progress: Regularly track your debt payoff progress to stay motivated and celebrate milestones along the way.

Seek Professional Advice: If debt is overwhelming, consider seeking advice from a financial counselor or advisor. They can provide guidance tailored to your specific situation.

Mapping Out a Long-Term Financial Plan

Creating a comprehensive long-term financial plan is essential for achieving financial independence. This plan serves as a roadmap that guides individuals toward their desired financial goals, helping them navigate various stages of life with confidence and purpose. Here's an in-depth exploration of how to map out a long-term financial plan:

Set Clear Goals: Defining your financial goals, both short-term and long-term, is the foundation of a successful financial plan. These goals could include paying off debt, saving for a home, funding education, achieving financial independence, and retirement.

Assess Current Financial Situation: Take stock of your current financial position. Evaluate your assets, liabilities, income, expenses, savings, investments, and debts. This provides a baseline for creating your plan.

Create a Budget: Develop a detailed budget that outlines your income, expenses, and savings goals. This budget will help you allocate funds for various purposes and manage your cash flow effectively.

Prioritize Debt Repayment: If you have existing debts, prioritize creating a strategy for paying them off. Consider using approaches like the debt snowball or debt avalanche methods to accelerate the repayment process.

Emergency Fund: Build and maintain an emergency fund with three to six months' worth of living expenses. This fund acts as a safety net during unexpected financial challenges.

Investment Strategy: Develop an investment strategy that aligns with your risk tolerance and long-term goals. Consider diversifying your investments across different asset classes to manage risk.

Retirement Planning: Determine how much you need for a comfortable retirement. Contribute regularly to retirement accounts such as 401(k)s or IRAs and take advantage of employer matching contributions.

Insurance Coverage: Review your insurance coverage, including health, life, disability, and property insurance. Adequate coverage protects you and your loved ones from unforeseen events.

Estate Planning: Create or update your estate plan, including a will, trust, and designation of beneficiaries. This ensures that your assets are distributed according to your wishes.

Regular Review: Regularly review and adjust your financial plan as your circumstances change. Life events, economic conditions, and personal goals may necessitate updates to your plan.

Professional Guidance: Consider seeking advice from financial advisors or planners. Their expertise can help you optimize your financial strategies and stay on track to meet your goals.

Adaptability and Flexibility: Stay adaptable and flexible as you execute your financial plan. Life is dynamic, and adjustments may be needed along the way.

A well-structured long-term financial plan sets the stage for achieving financial independence and realizing your aspirations. By following these steps and staying committed to your plan, you can navigate your financial journey with confidence and build a secure and prosperous future.

Passive vs. Active Income Streams

Understanding the distinction between passive and active income streams is pivotal on the path to financial independence. These two types of income play different roles in building wealth and achieving financial freedom. Here's a comprehensive exploration of passive and active income streams:

Active Income: Active income refers to money earned through active participation or effort in exchange for goods or services. It's income derived from your direct involvement in tasks, employment, or business activities. Here are the key aspects of active income:

Employment Income:

- Earnings received from a traditional job or occupation where you exchange time and skills for a paycheck.

Business Income:

- Income generated from running a business or providing services where your active involvement is necessary.

Freelancing and Consulting:

- Earnings from offering specialized services or expertise on a freelance or consulting basis.

Hourly or Salary Compensation:

- Income earned based on an hourly wage or fixed annual salary for work performed.

Direct Effort Required:

- Active income requires continuous effort, time, and direct involvement to generate earnings.

Limited Scalability:

- Active income streams often have limitations in terms of how much you can earn since your time and energy are finite.

Passive Income: Passive income refers to money earned with minimal ongoing effort or involvement after the initial setup. It's income that continues to flow without the need for constant attention. Here are the key aspects of passive income:

Rental Income:

- Earnings from renting out properties, such as real estate or land, without needing constant hands-on management.

Dividend Income:

- Earnings received from owning stocks or shares in companies that distribute a portion of their profits to shareholders.

Interest Income:

- Income earned from investments like bonds, certificates of deposit, or savings accounts.

Royalties:

- Earnings from creative works, such as books, music, patents, or intellectual property, when others use or buy them.

Automated Businesses:

- Income generated from businesses that can operate with minimal day-to-day involvement once set up, such as e-commerce stores.

Limited Involvement:

- Passive income requires upfront effort and investment, but ongoing management is minimal compared to active income.

Scalability and Flexibility:

- Passive income streams can be scalable and have the potential for greater earnings growth without a linear increase in effort.

Both passive and active income have their roles in achieving financial independence. Active income can provide immediate stability, while passive income offers long-term financial security and the potential to enjoy more freedom and flexibility in the future.

Diversification Strategies for Income

Diversifying income sources is a key strategy for achieving financial independence and resilience. Relying on a variety of income streams reduces risk, enhances financial stability, and provides a buffer against economic uncertainties. Here's a comprehensive exploration of diversification strategies for income:

Multiple Active Income Streams: Pursue various active income sources, such as part-time jobs, freelance work, consulting, or side businesses. Diversifying your active income streams reduces dependence on a single source of employment.

Passive Income Sources: Build a portfolio of passive income sources, including rental properties, dividend-paying stocks, interest-bearing investments, and royalties from intellectual property. Passive income requires upfront effort but can provide consistent earnings with minimal ongoing involvement.

Real Estate Investments: Consider investing in real estate properties for rental income. Real estate can provide a steady stream of cash flow and potential appreciation over time.

Dividend Stocks: Invest in dividend-paying stocks from reputable companies. Dividends can provide regular income while also participating in potential stock price appreciation.

Peer-to-Peer Lending: Explore peer-to-peer lending platforms where you can lend money to individuals or small businesses in exchange for interest payments.

Create Online Courses or Products: Leverage your expertise by creating and selling online courses, e-books, or digital products. Once developed, these products can generate passive income.

Invest in Bonds: Invest in bonds, which pay interest over a fixed period. Bonds are generally considered more stable than stocks and can provide consistent income.

Annuities: Consider annuities, which are financial products that provide a stream of income over a specified period, often used for retirement income.

Royalties and Licensing: If you have creative works or intellectual property, license them for royalties. This can include books, music, art, or software.

Affiliate Marketing: Participate in affiliate marketing by promoting products or services and earning a commission for each sale made through your referral.

E-commerce and Dropshipping: Start an e-commerce store or engage in dropshipping, where you sell products online without the need to maintain inventory.

Build an Investment Portfolio: Create a diversified investment portfolio that includes stocks, bonds, real estate investment trusts (REITs), and other assets to generate a mix of income sources.

Explore Entrepreneurial Ventures: Identify entrepreneurial opportunities that align with your skills and interests. These ventures can range from online ventures to local businesses.

Regularly Monitor and Adjust: Regularly review the performance of your income sources and make adjustments as needed. Economic conditions and market trends may require shifts in your income strategy.

Emergency Fund and Savings: Maintain an emergency fund to cover unexpected expenses and income disruptions. Having a financial safety net is crucial for sustaining your income diversification strategy.

By diversifying your income sources, you can create a more stable and resilient financial foundation. This approach minimizes dependency on a single source of income and enhances your ability to achieve financial independence and weather economic fluctuations.

Exploring Real Estate Investments

Real estate investments have long been considered a tangible and potentially lucrative way to build wealth and achieve financial independence. They offer opportunities for rental income, property appreciation, and portfolio diversification. Here's an in-depth exploration of real estate investments:

Types of Real Estate Investments:

- Residential Properties: These include single-family homes, condos, and apartment buildings that are rented out to tenants.
- Commercial Properties: Commercial real estate encompasses office buildings, retail spaces, warehouses, and industrial properties.
- Real Estate Investment Trusts (REITs): REITs are companies that own, operate, or finance income-generating real estate across various sectors.

Benefits of Real Estate Investments:

- Rental Income: Rental properties provide a consistent stream of income from tenants' monthly payments.
- Property Appreciation: Real estate has the potential to appreciate in value over time, increasing your investment's worth.
- Portfolio Diversification: Real estate offers diversification, reducing risk by balancing your investment portfolio.
- Leverage: Real estate allows you to leverage your investment by financing a portion and using borrowed funds.

Key Considerations Before Investing:

- Market Research: Analyze local real estate markets to understand property demand, rental rates, and potential for appreciation.
- Financing Options: Explore mortgage rates, down payment requirements, and loan terms to determine the most suitable financing option.

- Property Management: Decide whether to manage the property yourself or hire a property management company to handle tenant relations, maintenance, and rent collection.
- Location: Location significantly impacts property value and rental demand. Choose areas with growth potential and amenities.
- Cash Flow Analysis: Calculate potential rental income and subtract expenses like mortgage payments, property taxes, insurance, and maintenance to assess cash flow.

Rental Property Strategies:

- Buy and Hold: Purchase properties with the intention of renting them out for a steady stream of rental income and long-term appreciation.
- House Hacking: Live in one unit of a multi-unit property while renting out the others to cover your mortgage and expenses.
- Vacation Rentals: Invest in properties located in tourist destinations and rent them out to vacationers through platforms like Airbnb.

Flipping Properties:

- Property Flipping: Buy properties at a lower price, renovate or improve them, and then sell them for a profit.
- Renovation Costs: Calculate renovation costs accurately to ensure your projected profit margin remains feasible.

Real Estate Investment Trusts (REITs):

- Passive Investment: Invest in REITs to gain exposure to real estate without directly owning properties.
- Dividend Income: REITs distribute a significant portion of their earnings as dividends to shareholders.
- Liquidity: REITs are publicly traded, providing ease of entry and exit for investors.

Risks and Mitigation:

- Market Volatility: Real estate markets can experience fluctuations, affecting property values and rental demand.
- Property Management Challenges: Poor management can lead to tenant issues, vacancies, and higher maintenance costs.
- Interest Rate Changes: Rising interest rates can impact mortgage payments and profitability.
- Location Risk: Investing in declining or stagnant areas may result in limited appreciation potential.

Due Diligence and Education:

- Research: Conduct thorough research on potential properties, local market trends, and investment strategies.
- Education: Stay informed about real estate investing through books, courses, seminars, and networking with experienced investors.

Long-Term Strategy:

- Patience: Real estate investing often requires a long-term perspective to fully realize benefits like appreciation and equity buildup.
- Exit Strategy: Plan your exit strategy in advance, whether it involves selling, holding, or passing on properties.

Real estate investments offer a compelling opportunity to generate income, build equity, and diversify your investment portfolio. By carefully considering your goals, conducting due diligence, and understanding the local market dynamics, you can make informed decisions that align with your financial objectives and pave the way toward greater financial independence.

Creating and Selling Online Courses or Ebooks

In the digital age, creating and selling online courses or ebooks has emerged as a powerful way to generate income, share expertise, and establish yourself as an authority in your field. Leveraging your knowledge and skills, you can create valuable content that resonates with your audience and contributes to your financial independence. Here's a comprehensive exploration of creating and selling online courses or ebooks:

Identify Your Expertise: Determine your area of expertise, whether it's a skill, knowledge, or passion that you can effectively teach others.

Market Research: Research your target audience's needs, preferences, and pain points. Understand what information they are seeking and how you can address their challenges.

Content Creation: Develop high-quality content that addresses your audience's needs. This can include written materials, video lessons, audio recordings, worksheets, and more.

Choose a Platform: Select a platform for hosting and delivering your online course or ebook. Popular options include Udemy, Teachable, Thinkific, and Amazon Kindle Direct Publishing for ebooks.

Structuring Your Content: Organize your content into well-structured modules or chapters. Create a clear outline that guides learners through the learning journey.

Engaging Content Delivery: Use a variety of formats such as videos, slideshows, quizzes, and interactive activities to keep learners engaged and enhance their understanding.

Quality and Professionalism: Ensure your content is well-produced and professional. Invest in good audio, video, and graphic quality to provide a positive learning experience.

Pricing Strategy: Determine the pricing for your course or ebook. Consider factors like the value you're providing, competitor pricing, and your target audience's budget.

Marketing and Promotion: Develop a marketing strategy to reach your target audience. Utilize social media, email marketing, content marketing, and collaborations to promote your offerings.

Build a Website or Landing Page: Create a dedicated website or landing page for your course or ebook. This provides a central hub for information and purchasing.

Optimize for SEO: If selling ebooks, optimize your book's title, description, and keywords for search engines to improve discoverability on platforms like Amazon.

Leverage Existing Audience: If you have an existing online presence or following, leverage it to promote your course or ebook to an already-engaged audience.

Collect and Incorporate Feedback: Listen to feedback from your early customers and learners. Use their input to improve and enhance your offerings.

Continuous Updates: Keep your content up-to-date and relevant. This demonstrates your commitment to quality and encourages repeat purchases.

Protect Your Intellectual Property: If selling ebooks, ensure you have copyright protection for your work to prevent unauthorized distribution.

Measure and Analyze: Track metrics like sales, engagement, and learner feedback. Use this data to refine your offerings and marketing strategies.

Creating and selling online courses or ebooks can be a fulfilling endeavor that generates passive income and builds your personal brand. With dedication, continuous improvement, and a focus on delivering value, you can establish a revenue stream that contributes to your financial independence.

Leveraging Investments in Dividend Stocks

Investing in dividend stocks is a strategic approach to building a passive income stream that can contribute to financial independence. Dividend stocks offer the potential for both capital appreciation and regular dividend payments, making them an attractive option for investors seeking income stability and growth. Here's a comprehensive exploration of leveraging investments in dividend stocks:

Identifying Dividend Stocks:

- Identifying dividend stocks requires thorough research and consideration. Look for companies with a proven history of consistent dividend payments. Focus on stable and reputable companies spanning various sectors to diversify your portfolio effectively.

Dividend Yield and Payout Ratio:

- Analyze the dividend yield, which represents the annual dividend payment as a percentage of the stock's current price. Also, assess the payout ratio, which indicates the proportion of earnings allocated to dividends. A sustainable yield and reasonable payout ratio are indicators of a company's financial health.

Dividend Growth History:

- Study a company's track record of dividend growth. Consistent increases in dividends over time signal a company's financial stability and commitment to rewarding shareholders. This history underscores the company's potential for long-term value.

Reinvestment Plans:

- Consider dividend reinvestment plans (DRIPs) that enable you to automatically reinvest dividends to purchase more shares. DRIPs contribute to compounding returns over time, boosting the growth of your investment.

Portfolio Diversification:

- Diversifying your dividend stock portfolio across different sectors and industries is crucial. This diversification reduces risk and enhances stability, protecting your investments from industry-specific downturns.

Long-Term Investment Perspective:

- Approach dividend stock investing with a long-term perspective. Dividend stocks tend to benefit significantly from the power of compounding, which amplifies returns over extended periods.

Dividend Aristocrats and Kings:

- Consider companies designated as Dividend Aristocrats or Kings. These are businesses with an impressive track record of increasing dividends for a specified number of consecutive years (e.g., Dividend Aristocrats have at least 25 years of dividend growth). Such companies often display strong financial management.

Dividend ETFs and Funds:

- If individual stock selection seems daunting, explore dividend-focused exchange-traded funds (ETFs) and mutual funds. These vehicles provide diversification across a basket of dividend-paying stocks, minimizing risk.

Tax Considerations:

- Understand the tax implications of dividend income. Dividends can be subject to different tax rates based on factors like your country of residence and the type of account you hold. Seek tax-efficient strategies to maximize your after-tax returns.

Monitoring Company Performance:

- Continuously monitor the financial health and performance of the companies in your dividend stock portfolio. Stay informed about changes in earnings, market trends, and other factors that could impact dividend sustainability.

Buy and Hold Strategy:

- Embrace a buy and hold strategy for dividend stocks. Frequent trading can erode gains through transaction costs and potential capital gains taxes. Holding onto dividend stocks over the long term allows you to benefit from compounding returns.

Dividend Capture Strategy:

- Implement a dividend capture strategy if you seek short-term gains from dividend payouts without holding the stock for an extended period. This strategy involves buying a stock just before the ex-dividend date and selling shortly after.

Economic and Market Conditions:

- Be mindful of economic cycles and market conditions that can influence dividend stocks. Economic downturns may affect companies' ability to maintain dividend payments. Understanding the broader economic landscape helps you make informed decisions.

Reinvest Dividends or Receive Cash:

- Decide whether to reinvest dividends to compound your returns or receive them as cash for income. Your decision depends on your financial goals and current income needs.

Regular Portfolio Review:

- Regularly review and adjust your dividend stock portfolio based on changes in company fundamentals, market trends, and your own financial objectives. Flexibility ensures your portfolio remains aligned with your goals.

Staying Informed:

- Stay well-informed about the companies you invest in, industry trends, and broader economic factors that can impact dividend stocks. Being knowledgeable empowers you to make informed decisions and adapt to changing circumstances effectively.

Investing in dividend stocks can be a rewarding strategy for generating passive income and building wealth over time. By selecting solid dividend-paying companies, maintaining a diversified portfolio, and staying committed to a long-term investment approach, you can leverage the power of dividend stocks to contribute to your journey toward financial independence.

Embracing a Minimalist Lifestyle

Adopting a minimalist lifestyle can be a transformative journey toward achieving financial independence, reducing stress, and finding contentment in simplicity. By consciously simplifying your possessions, commitments, and consumption habits, you can focus on what truly matters and allocate resources toward your financial goals. Here's a comprehensive exploration of embracing a minimalist lifestyle:

Understanding Minimalism:

- Minimalism is more than just a design aesthetic; it's a mindset that prioritizes quality over quantity and aims to simplify life in all its facets. It involves decluttering physical, mental, and emotional spaces to create room for what truly matters. At its core, minimalism encourages intentionality and conscious living.

Clarify Your Values:

- To embrace minimalism, start by clarifying your values. Reflect deeply on what truly brings you joy, fulfillment, and purpose. Identifying your core values helps guide your decisions and ensures that your actions align with what matters most to you.

Declutter Your Space:

- The physical aspect of minimalism begins with decluttering your living spaces. Go through your belongings and keep only items that are functional, meaningful, and aligned with your values. This process not only creates an organized environment but also reduces visual and mental clutter.

Reducing Material Possessions:

- Adopt intentional consumerism by focusing on buying items that serve a purpose and add value to your life. Minimalism encourages you to avoid accumulating excessive possessions and instead choose quality over quantity.

Mindful Consumption:

- Before making a purchase, practice mindful consumption. Ask yourself whether the item truly aligns with your needs and values. Consider its long-term utility and impact on your life. Mindful buying prevents impulse purchases and promotes a more intentional approach to consumption.

Digital Minimalism:

- Minimalism extends to your digital life as well. Digital minimalism involves decluttering your digital devices, unsubscribing from unnecessary emails, and managing your online presence. By curating your digital world, you create a more focused and intentional online experience.

Embrace Experiences:

- Minimalism encourages you to prioritize experiences over material possessions. Invest in activities that create lasting memories, enrich your life, and foster meaningful connections with others. These experiences contribute to a sense of fulfillment and well-being.

Streamline Commitments:

- Evaluate your commitments and obligations with a minimalist lens. Focus on those that align with your goals and values, and consider letting go of those that drain your time and energy without significant benefit.

Financial Benefits:

- Minimalism can have positive financial implications. By reducing unnecessary spending, prioritizing value-driven purchases, and embracing a simpler lifestyle, you can lower expenses, increase savings, and make more mindful financial decisions.

Reduce Environmental Impact:

- Minimalism aligns with environmental sustainability. Consuming less leads to a smaller carbon footprint and reduced waste. By valuing quality over quantity, you contribute to a more eco-friendly way of living.

Mindful Spending:

- Mindful spending is a key aspect of minimalism. It involves considering the long-term value of your purchases and avoiding impulsive buying. By practicing mindful spending, you cultivate a deeper awareness of the impact of your choices.

Quality Over Quantity:

- Opting for quality over quantity is a fundamental principle of minimalism. Instead of accumulating a large quantity of items, focus on acquiring high-quality possessions that are durable and serve their purpose effectively.

Digital Detox:

- Regularly disconnecting from digital devices through a digital detox allows you to recharge, foster presence, nurture creativity, and engage in meaningful face-to-face interactions.

Emotional Well-being:

- Minimalism can have a profound impact on your emotional well-being. By simplifying your surroundings and reducing visual clutter, you may experience reduced stress, increased focus, and an overall improved mental state.

Create Space for What Matters:

- Clearing physical and mental clutter creates space for activities, relationships, and pursuits that truly bring you joy and fulfillment. Minimalism empowers you to curate your life to align with your aspirations.

Practice Gratitude:

- Minimalism encourages you to shift your focus from constantly seeking more to cultivating gratitude for what you already have. Embracing gratitude enhances your contentment and appreciation for the present moment.

Educate Yourself:

- Deepen your commitment to minimalism by educating yourself. Read books, watch documentaries, and follow minimalist bloggers to gain insights, perspectives, and practical tips for incorporating minimalism into your life.

Simplify Routines:

- Minimalism extends to simplifying your daily routines. By streamlining habits and decision-making processes, you reduce decision fatigue and create a more peaceful, intentional, and efficient life.

Community and Support:

- Connecting with a community of like-minded individuals who embrace minimalism can be motivating and inspiring. Sharing experiences, tips, and challenges creates a sense of belonging and reinforces your commitment to a simpler lifestyle.

By embracing these principles of minimalism, you can create a life that is more intentional, purposeful, and aligned with your values. Whether you're seeking to declutter your physical spaces, streamline your commitments, or cultivate gratitude, minimalism offers a holistic approach to living a more meaningful and fulfilling life.

- .

Embracing a minimalist lifestyle is a deliberate choice to focus on what truly matters and eliminate distractions. By simplifying your surroundings, reducing clutter, and aligning your actions with your values, you can create a life that is intentional, fulfilling, and aligned with your journey toward financial independence.

Strategies for Cutting Unnecessary Expenses

Assess Your Current Spending:

Reviewing your bank statements, credit card bills, and receipts provides a comprehensive snapshot of your financial habits. It reveals where your money is going and helps you identify spending patterns. This awareness is essential for making informed decisions about which expenses to cut. It's often surprising to discover how small, recurring purchases can accumulate over time, impacting your overall financial health.

Categorize Expenses:

Categorizing expenses into essential and non-essential categories helps you prioritize your spending. Essential expenses include items like housing, groceries, and utilities that are necessary for your basic needs. Non-essential expenses encompass things like entertainment, dining out, and impulse purchases. This categorization allows you to evaluate where you have room to cut back without sacrificing necessities.

Create a Budget:

Developing a budget is a foundational step in managing your finances effectively. A budget allocates specific amounts for each spending category, including essentials and discretionary spending. It provides clear boundaries and prevents overspending. When creating a budget, consider your income, financial goals, and existing expenses. Setting limits on discretionary spending encourages you to be intentional about where your money goes.

Prioritize Financial Goals:

Understanding your financial goals is essential for making informed spending decisions. Whether you're focused on paying off debt, building an emergency fund, or saving for investments, prioritizing these goals helps you align your spending with your aspirations. When faced with a spending choice, you can assess whether it brings you closer to or farther from your financial objectives.

Track Daily Spending:

Daily spending can easily accumulate without your notice. Keeping track of small expenses, such as coffee, snacks, or impulse purchases, helps you identify areas where you might be overspending. Using apps or journals to record your spending habits in real time provides a tangible record that promotes mindfulness and accountability.

Implement the 30-Day Rule:

The 30-day rule introduces a cooling-off period for non-essential purchases. Instead of acting on impulse, wait for 30 days before buying. This rule helps you distinguish between fleeting desires and genuine needs. Often, after the waiting period, you might find that the urge to buy has subsided, allowing you to save money by avoiding unnecessary purchases.

Meal Planning and Cooking at Home:

Preparing meals at home offers multiple benefits. It's not only cost-effective but also promotes healthier eating habits. Planning your meals and cooking at home reduces the temptation to dine out frequently, saving you money on restaurant bills and takeout. Moreover, meal planning can help you reduce food wastage by buying only what you need.

Cut Subscription Services:

Subscription services can silently drain your finances. Evaluate the value of each subscription, and cancel those you rarely use or that no longer align with your interests. Whether it's streaming services, magazine subscriptions, or memberships, eliminating unnecessary subscriptions can lead to substantial savings over time.

Negotiate Bills:

Service providers often have room for negotiation on rates. Contact your utility, cable, internet, and insurance providers to inquire about potential discounts or promotions. A simple phone call can result in lowered bills, helping you save money without sacrificing quality or essential services.

Use Cash or Debit Cards:

Opting for cash or debit card payments can be an effective strategy for staying within your budget. When you use cash or debit, you're limited to the funds available, reducing the risk of accumulating credit card debt. This practice encourages conscious spending and discourages overspending.

Automate Savings:

Setting up automated transfers to savings or investment accounts right after receiving your paycheck ensures that you prioritize saving before discretionary spending. This "pay yourself first" approach reinforces the habit of saving and investing, making progress toward your financial goals a consistent practice.

Shop Mindfully:

Shopping mindfully involves making deliberate and intentional purchasing decisions. Before buying something, ask yourself if the item truly aligns with your needs and values. By avoiding impulse buys and being selective about what you purchase, you can significantly cut down on unnecessary spending.

Comparison Shopping:

Comparison shopping involves researching and comparing prices, features, and options before making a purchase. Whether you're buying electronics, appliances, or even groceries, taking the time to compare can help you find the best deals and make informed choices that align with your budget.

Buy Used or Secondhand:

Consider buying used or secondhand items for items that have a short lifespan or items that are still in excellent condition. This approach can save you money on items like clothing, electronics, furniture, and more, without sacrificing quality.

Downsize and Declutter:

Assess your belongings regularly and consider selling, donating, or recycling items you no longer use or need. Downsizing and decluttering not only help you create a more organized living space but also generate extra funds by selling items you no longer require.

Limit Entertainment Spending:

Finding free or low-cost entertainment options can significantly cut down your entertainment expenses. Participate in community events, explore local parks, engage in DIY projects, or plan budget-friendly outings with friends. These alternatives provide enjoyment without straining your budget.

Limit Online Shopping:

Unsubscribing from shopping emails and avoiding online browsing helps reduce the temptation to make impulsive online purchases. By minimizing exposure to online shopping platforms, you can prevent unnecessary spending and focus on mindful consumption.

DIY Projects:

Taking on do-it-yourself (DIY) projects for home improvement, repairs, and simple renovations can save you money on hiring professionals. Learning basic skills and tackling projects yourself can be rewarding and cost-effective.

Energy Efficiency:

Energy-efficient habits, such as using energy-efficient appliances, turning off lights when not needed, and reducing water consumption, contribute to lower utility bills. These small changes accumulate over time and lead to significant savings.

Reduce Transportation Costs:

Exploring alternative transportation options like carpooling, using public transportation, biking, or walking can help you cut commuting expenses. Not only does this save you money on fuel and maintenance but it can also contribute to a greener lifestyle.

Socialize Frugally:

Instead of costly activities, plan budget-friendly outings with friends, like picnics, potlucks, game nights, or group hikes. These social activities foster connections without straining your finances.

Practice Contentment:

Cultivating contentment involves appreciating what you have and finding joy in experiences and relationships rather than material possessions. This mindset shift reduces the inclination for constant consumerism and leads to more intentional spending.

Regular Expense Review:

Periodically reviewing your budget and expenses helps you identify any creeping unnecessary spending. As your circumstances change, your spending priorities might need adjustment. Regular review ensures that your spending aligns with your current financial goals.

Celebrate Progress:

Celebrating milestones as you cut expenses and make progress toward your financial goals reinforces positive behaviors. Acknowledging your efforts can motivate you to continue making intentional financial decisions.

By applying these strategies to your daily life, you can effectively cut unnecessary expenses and allocate more resources toward your financial goals. Each small step you take brings you closer to achieving financial independence and a more mindful relationship with your finances.

Mindful Spending: Aligning Expenses with Values

Mindful spending goes beyond the mere act of purchasing. It involves a thoughtful approach to financial decisions, where each expense is evaluated in the context of your values, goals, and overall well-being. By adopting this practice, you can ensure that your spending aligns with what truly matters to you, leading to greater satisfaction, reduced financial stress, and a more intentional approach to your finances.

Understanding Mindful Spending:

Mindful spending is rooted in the idea that every purchase should reflect your core values and contribute to your well-being. It's about breaking away from the cycle of impulsive buying driven by advertisements or societal pressure and instead making choices that resonate with your beliefs and aspirations. This practice helps you regain control over your finances and empowers you to use your money in ways that bring genuine contentment.

Identify Your Values:

To embark on the journey of mindful spending, start by identifying your values. What matters most to you in life? Is it family, health, personal growth, experiences, or giving back to the community? By understanding your values, you can set the foundation for aligning your expenses with what truly brings you joy and fulfillment.

Prioritize Spending Categories:

Categorizing your spending helps you allocate resources where they matter most. Divide your expenses into categories like essential needs (housing, food, utilities), personal growth (education, hobbies), experiences (travel, leisure), and contributions (charitable giving). This segmentation allows you to allocate funds according to your priorities, ensuring that your spending reflects your values.

Eliminate Impulse Buying:

Mindful spending urges you to resist the allure of impulse buying. It encourages you to pause before making a purchase and consider whether it aligns with your values and contributes positively to your life. By avoiding impulsive purchases, you can prevent buyer's remorse and redirect resources toward things that have a lasting impact.

Pause and Reflect:

Before making a purchase, take a moment to reflect. Ask yourself why you're making the purchase and how it fits into your values and goals. Is it a need or a want? Will it enhance your life in a meaningful way? This reflection allows you to make decisions with a clear understanding of the implications.

Avoid Emotional Spending:

Emotional spending occurs when emotions like stress, boredom, or sadness drive purchasing decisions. Mindful spending encourages you to recognize these triggers and find healthier alternatives to address emotional needs. Rather than seeking temporary relief through shopping, you can channel your emotions into activities that align with your values, such as exercise, meditation, or spending quality time with loved ones.

Embrace Quality Over Quantity:

Mindful spending often involves embracing quality over quantity. Instead of accumulating numerous possessions, you focus on acquiring items that align with your values and serve a meaningful purpose. This shift can lead to a simpler and more purposeful life, where each possession brings value and significance.

Practice Gratitude:

Mindful spending promotes gratitude by encouraging you to appreciate what you have. When you align your expenses with your values, you develop a deeper sense of contentment and gratitude for the experiences, possessions, and opportunities that truly matter to you.

Long-Term Fulfillment:

By aligning your expenses with your values, you invest in experiences and possessions that contribute to your long-term fulfillment. This approach reduces the accumulation of things that provide fleeting satisfaction and fosters a sense of purpose and meaning in your financial choices.

Enhanced Financial Well-Being:

Mindful spending positively impacts your financial well-being. By curbing unnecessary expenses and focusing on what matters most, you free up resources to achieve your goals, whether it's building an emergency fund, investing, or pursuing personal passions.

Creating Positive Habits:

Mindful spending isn't a one-time action; it's a habit that you cultivate over time. By consistently evaluating your purchases, making intentional choices, and reflecting on the alignment with your values, you create a positive cycle of conscious consumption.

Contribution to Financial Independence:

Mindful spending is a key contributor to achieving financial independence. By directing your resources toward what truly matters, you maximize your savings, reduce wasteful spending, and create a strong foundation for your financial future.

Holistic Well-Being:

Mindful spending extends beyond financial considerations. It promotes holistic well-being by ensuring that your choices align with your mental, emotional, and physical health, fostering a balanced and harmonious life.

Embracing mindful spending is a powerful way to transform your relationship with money. By intentionally evaluating and aligning your expenses with your values, you can achieve greater satisfaction, make informed financial decisions, and move closer to realizing your financial independence and life aspirations.

Benefits of Downsizing and Decluttering

Downsizing and decluttering are transformative practices that extend far beyond the physical act of tidying up. These processes involve intentionally simplifying your living environment and possessions, resulting in a multitude of benefits that positively impact various aspects of your life. From reducing stress to enhancing productivity, here's a comprehensive exploration of the benefits of downsizing and decluttering:

Enhanced Clarity and Focus:

- When your living space is free from clutter, your mind can operate with enhanced clarity and focus. Without the distraction of disorder, you can think more clearly, make decisions more easily, and concentrate on tasks with increased efficiency.

Reduced Stress and Anxiety:

- Clutter has a direct impact on your mental well-being. A cluttered environment can lead to heightened stress and anxiety, while decluttering promotes a sense of calm and tranquility. A simplified space reduces visual noise, helping to alleviate stress and create a more serene atmosphere.

Simplified Daily Routine:

- Downsizing and decluttering simplify your daily routine. With fewer possessions to manage, you spend less time searching for items and maintaining your space. This streamlined approach to daily life leaves you with more time and energy to dedicate to meaningful activities.

More Space and Freedom:

- Downsizing creates physical space in your home, fostering a sense of freedom and expansiveness. This newfound space not only improves the overall aesthetics of your living area but also offers room to move, breathe, and engage in activities that bring you joy.

Increased Productivity:

- An organized environment directly influences your productivity. When your belongings are organized and easily accessible, you can complete tasks more efficiently. This is particularly beneficial for both your personal and professional pursuits, helping you achieve your goals with greater ease.

Financial Savings:

- Downsizing can have significant financial benefits. If you choose to downsize your living space, you can potentially reduce housing costs, property taxes, and utility bills. Moreover, decluttering prevents unnecessary spending on items you already have or no longer need.

Positive Environmental Impact:

- Decluttering leads to a reduction in waste. By disposing of items you no longer require, you contribute to a more sustainable lifestyle. Additionally, the conscious consumption encouraged by decluttering reduces the demand for new goods, which can help mitigate environmental strain.

Easier Maintenance:

- A clutter-free environment requires less maintenance and cleaning. With fewer items to dust, organize, and clean, you save time and effort in keeping your living space neat and tidy.

Facilitated Decision-Making:

- When you have fewer possessions, making decisions becomes easier. The abundance of choices that clutter can bring can often lead to decision paralysis. Decluttering streamlines your choices and promotes a more efficient decision-making process.

Enhanced Creativity:

- A clutter-free environment fosters creativity. The absence of visual clutter allows your mind to roam freely and encourages creative thinking. Whether you're pursuing artistic endeavors or problem-solving in your work, a decluttered space can enhance your innovative thinking.

Improved Relationships:

- A clutter-free home promotes harmonious relationships among family members or housemates. An organized space reduces tension and stress associated with a chaotic environment, contributing to a more peaceful coexistence.

Mindfulness and Intention:

- The act of decluttering encourages mindfulness and intentionality. It prompts you to evaluate each possession and its significance in your life. This deliberate consideration cultivates a deeper awareness of what truly matters to you.

A Sense of Accomplishment:

- Completing the process of downsizing and decluttering often brings a sense of accomplishment. Clearing your space and letting go of items can boost your self-esteem and provide a psychological lift.

Smooth Transitions:

- Downsizing can be particularly beneficial during transitional phases in life, such as moving to a new home, retiring, or transitioning to an empty nest. A more compact living situation can make these transitions smoother and less overwhelming.

Focus on Experiences:

- As you declutter and downsize, you naturally shift your focus from material possessions to experiences. This change in perspective encourages you to seek happiness and fulfillment in meaningful experiences rather than in accumulating things.

Easier Relocation:

- When you have fewer belongings, relocating becomes more straightforward. Packing and unpacking are less time-consuming and stressful, allowing for a smoother transition to a new living space.

Promotion of Gratitude:

- A decluttered living space promotes gratitude. By owning fewer items, you develop a deeper appreciation for what you have and are more likely to care for and maintain your possessions.

Enhanced Energy Flow:

- Feng Shui and other philosophies emphasize the importance of unobstructed energy flow in a space. Decluttering encourages positive energy circulation, creating a more balanced and harmonious environment.

Promotion of Minimalism:

- Downsizing and decluttering are inherent to the minimalist lifestyle. Minimalism advocates for owning only what adds value to your life, encouraging you to focus on quality rather than quantity.

Freedom to Travel:

- With fewer possessions to tie you down, you gain greater freedom to travel and explore. You can embark on spontaneous trips without the burden of excessive belongings.

Encouragement of Mindful Purchases:

- Once you've experienced the benefits of downsizing and decluttering, you become more mindful of future purchases. You're more likely to think twice before acquiring new possessions, ensuring that they truly align with your values and needs.

Cultivation of Contentment:

- Downsizing fosters contentment by showing you that happiness isn't derived solely from material possessions. The realization that you can thrive with less can lead to greater contentment in your daily life.

Contribution to Financial Independence:

- The financial savings resulting from downsizing and decluttering can be redirected toward your financial goals, such as building an emergency fund, paying off debt, or investing for the future.

Holistic Well-Being:

- The holistic benefits of downsizing and decluttering extend to your mental, emotional, and physical well-being. An organized and simplified living environment positively impacts various aspects of your life.

Incorporating downsizing and decluttering into your lifestyle can have profound and lasting effects. By intentionally simplifying your surroundings, you create space for growth, creativity, and fulfillment. The benefits go beyond the physical realm, touching every facet of your well-being and contributing to a more intentional and purposeful life.

Minimalism's Impact on Mental Health and Well-being

Reduced Clutter and Stress:

- A cluttered environment can contribute to feelings of overwhelm and stress. Embracing minimalism by decluttering physical spaces helps create a more serene atmosphere, leading to reduced stress and anxiety. A tidy space fosters mental clarity and promotes a sense of calm.

Enhanced Focus and Productivity:

- Minimalism encourages you to eliminate distractions and unnecessary possessions. With fewer items vying for your attention, you can concentrate more effectively on tasks and goals. This enhanced focus boosts your productivity and allows you to accomplish more in less time.

Mindful Consumption and Intentionality:

- Practicing mindful consumption is a cornerstone of minimalism. By being intentional about what you bring into your life, you cultivate a deeper awareness of your needs and desires. This mindfulness extends beyond material possessions to your thoughts, relationships, and actions, contributing to a more conscious and purpose-driven life.

Freedom from Consumerism and Comparison:

- Consumerism often leads to a cycle of constant craving and comparison. Minimalism encourages you to break free from this cycle by valuing experiences over possessions and focusing on what truly brings you joy. Liberated from the pressure to accumulate things, you're more likely to find contentment in the present moment.

Emotional Resilience and Well-being:

- Simplifying your life through minimalism can enhance emotional resilience. Letting go of excess possessions and unnecessary commitments allows you to focus on what truly matters, leading to a more balanced emotional state. This emotional well-being translates into healthier relationships and an improved overall outlook on life.

Cultivation of Gratitude:

- Minimalism fosters a sense of gratitude for what you have. By appreciating the value in each possession and experience, you shift your focus from scarcity to abundance. This shift in perspective enhances your overall well-being and reinforces a positive mindset.

Less Decision Fatigue:

- Decision fatigue occurs when you're faced with an overwhelming number of choices. Minimalism helps alleviate this fatigue by simplifying your options. With fewer possessions and commitments to manage, you can make decisions more efficiently and with less mental strain.

Increased Space for Creativity:

- A clutter-free environment opens up physical and mental space for creativity to flourish. With fewer distractions and visual clutter, your mind is free to explore new ideas and solutions. This creative outlet can contribute to a greater sense of fulfillment and purpose.

Promotion of Mindful Living:

- Minimalism encourages you to live in the present moment and savor the experiences that matter most. By shedding unnecessary baggage—both physical and mental—you create room for mindful living, which supports overall mental health and well-being.

Strengthened Relationships:

- The pursuit of minimalism often leads to more meaningful and genuine relationships. As you focus on nurturing connections that truly matter, you're likely to experience deeper bonds and more authentic interactions, contributing to improved mental and emotional well-being.

Reduced Environmental Impact:

- By consuming less and being more mindful of your choices, minimalism promotes a reduced environmental footprint. This alignment with sustainable living can provide a sense of purpose and contribute to a greater sense of well-being as you make choices that positively impact the planet.

Mindful Reflection and Self-Discovery:

- Minimalism encourages self-reflection and self-discovery. As you pare down possessions and simplify your life, you gain insight into what truly resonates with your values and aspirations. This self-awareness contributes to personal growth and a deeper understanding of yourself.

Embracing Minimalist Habits:

- Incorporating minimalist habits into your daily routine, such as mindful consumption, decluttering, and intentional decision-making, reinforces positive mental health practices. Over time, these habits become ingrained, leading to sustained well-being and a more intentional way of life.

Improved Sleep and Relaxation:

- A clutter-free and organized environment can positively impact your sleep quality and relaxation. An uncluttered bedroom promotes a peaceful atmosphere conducive to restful sleep, while a clutter-free living space provides a haven for relaxation and rejuvenation.

Heightened Contentment and Fulfillment:

- Minimalism's focus on valuing experiences, relationships, and personal growth over material possessions can lead to a heightened sense of contentment and fulfillment. As you detach from the pursuit of consumerism, you find joy in simpler pleasures and enriching experiences.

Balance in Digital Consumption:

- Minimalism extends to your digital life as well. By curating your digital interactions and setting boundaries on screen time, you create a healthier balance between online and offline experiences. This balanced approach contributes to improved mental well-being and reduced digital-related stress.

Release from Mental Clutter:

- Minimalism isn't confined to physical spaces; it also extends to mental and emotional realms. By letting go of mental clutter, such as negative thought patterns and excessive worries, you free up mental space for positivity, mindfulness, and a more tranquil state of mind.

Respect for Your Well-being:

- Embracing minimalism is an act of self-respect. It acknowledges that your well-being is paramount and that simplifying your life—physically, mentally, and emotionally—supports your overall health and happiness.

Nurturing Mind-Body Connection:

- Minimalism promotes a harmonious mind-body connection by

reducing external distractions and stressors. This alignment enhances your ability to listen to your body's cues, practice self-care, and foster holistic well-being.

Incorporating minimalism into your life can yield a multitude of mental health benefits. From reducing stress and clutter to fostering gratitude and enhancing creativity, minimalism provides a framework for living with intention, purpose, and mindfulness—ultimately contributing to a more fulfilling and mentally balanced life.

The Power of Compound Interest

Foundation of Wealth Accumulation:

- Compound interest serves as the foundation of wealth accumulation. It's the concept of earning interest on both the initial investment and the accumulated interest over time. This compounding effect can significantly boost the growth of your investments.

Harnessing Time as an Ally:

- Time is a crucial factor in the power of compound interest. The longer your money remains invested, the more time it has to compound and grow exponentially. Starting early allows you to harness time as an ally, amplifying your returns over the long term.

Exponential Growth Over Time:

- Compound interest results in exponential growth over time. As your investment grows, the accumulated interest contributes to a larger base, leading to even more substantial interest earnings in subsequent periods. This compounding effect accelerates the growth of your wealth.

Snowball Effect of Returns:

- Compound interest creates a snowball effect of returns. Initially, your returns might seem modest, but as your investment accumulates, the interest generates a more significant impact. Over time, the snowball effect leads to substantial gains.

The Rule of 72:

- The Rule of 72 is a quick formula to estimate how long it takes for an investment to double in value based on a fixed annual rate of return.

By dividing 72 by the annual interest rate, you can approximate the number of years it takes for your investment to double through compounding.

Reinvestment of Earnings:

- Reinvesting your earnings—both interest and dividends—capitalizes on the power of compound interest. Instead of withdrawing gains, reinvesting them allows your investment to compound on a larger base, leading to faster and more substantial growth.

Consistency in Contributions:

- Consistently contributing to your investment over time amplifies the power of compound interest. Regular contributions provide more principal to compound and generate higher returns over the long run.

Long-Term Investment Horizon:

- Compound interest is most effective when viewed through a long-term investment horizon. It's not just about the initial interest earned but the compounding effect over years or decades that truly magnifies your returns.

Maximizing Retirement Savings:

- Compound interest is a cornerstone of retirement planning. By starting early and consistently contributing to retirement accounts like 401(k)s or IRAs, you can maximize the compounding effect, ensuring a more comfortable retirement lifestyle.

Financial Goal Achievement:

- Whether it's buying a home, funding education, or achieving any financial goal, compound interest can play a pivotal role. The earlier you begin investing, the more time you give your investments to grow and help you achieve your objectives.

Overcoming Market Volatility:

- Compound interest can help mitigate the impact of market volatility. While markets may experience fluctuations, the compounding effect over time smooths out short-term market variations and generates consistent long-term growth.

The Cost of Delay:

- Delaying investment can have a significant cost in terms of missed compounding opportunities. The longer you wait to start investing, the more you miss out on the exponential growth that compound interest offers.

Achieving Financial Independence:

- Compound interest is a key tool for achieving financial independence. It allows you to build wealth over time without relying solely on your active income. As your investments grow, they can generate passive income that supports your financial goals.

Empowerment Through Knowledge:

- Understanding the power of compound interest empowers you to make informed financial decisions. It motivates you to start investing early, consistently contribute, and prioritize long-term growth for a more secure financial future.

Comparison of Saving Strategies:

- Compound interest highlights the superiority of investment-based saving strategies over traditional savings methods. While interest on savings accounts remains relatively static, compound interest in investments leads to exponential growth.

Diversification and Risk Management:

- Diversifying your investment portfolio is essential for risk management. Compound interest encourages you to spread your investments across different asset classes, enhancing the potential for compounding growth while minimizing risks.

Educating Future Generations:

- Teaching the concept of compound interest to future generations instills the value of early investing and financial literacy. Understanding this concept empowers young individuals to make smart financial choices and secure their financial futures.

Balancing Risk and Return:

- Compound interest illustrates the balance between risk and return in investing. While higher returns typically come with higher risks, the compounding effect enables you to manage risk by generating substantial growth over time.

Holistic Financial Planning:

- Incorporating the power of compound interest into your financial plan ensures a holistic approach to wealth building. It encourages you to set long-term goals, adopt disciplined saving habits, and make strategic investment decisions for a prosperous future.

Understanding Different Investment Vehicles

Investing is a crucial aspect of wealth building and achieving financial goals. Various investment vehicles offer unique features, risk profiles, and potential returns. Understanding these options empowers investors to make informed decisions aligned with their financial objectives, risk tolerance, and time horizon.

Stocks:

- Stocks represent ownership in a company. When you buy shares of a company's stock, you become a shareholder and own a portion of the business. Stocks offer the potential for capital appreciation as the company grows and generates profits. However, they also come with higher volatility and risk due to market fluctuations.

Bonds:

- Bonds are debt securities issued by governments, municipalities, or corporations. When you invest in a bond, you're essentially lending money to the issuer in exchange for regular interest payments and the return of the principal amount at maturity. Bonds are generally considered lower risk than stocks but offer potentially lower returns.

Mutual Funds:

- Mutual funds pool money from multiple investors to invest in a diversified portfolio of stocks, bonds, or other assets. They offer diversification, professional management, and access to various markets. Investors buy shares in the mutual fund and share in the gains and losses of the underlying assets.

Exchange-Traded Funds (ETFs):

- ETFs are similar to mutual funds but trade on stock exchanges like individual stocks. They offer diversification, low fees, and flexibility. ETFs track an index, sector, or asset class and allow investors to buy and sell throughout the trading day.

Real Estate Investment Trusts (REITs):

- REITs are companies that own, operate, or finance income-generating real estate properties. By investing in REITs, you can gain exposure to the real estate market without owning physical properties. REITs offer regular dividends and potential capital appreciation.

Certificate of Deposit (CD):

- CDs are time deposits offered by banks with fixed terms and interest rates. They offer a predictable return and are considered low-risk investments. However, CDs have lower potential returns compared to other investment options.

Savings Accounts:

- Savings accounts are offered by banks and credit unions and provide a safe place to store money while earning interest. They are highly liquid but offer lower interest rates compared to other investment vehicles.

Commodities:

- Commodities include physical assets like gold, silver, oil, and agricultural products. Investing in commodities provides diversification and a hedge against inflation. However, commodity prices can be volatile and are influenced by global supply and demand.

Options:

- Options are derivatives that give investors the right, but not the obligation, to buy or sell an asset at a predetermined price within a specified timeframe. Options can be used for hedging, speculation, or generating income. They require a good understanding of market dynamics and risk management.

Cryptocurrencies:

- Cryptocurrencies are digital or virtual currencies that use cryptography for security. Bitcoin, Ethereum, and other cryptocurrencies have gained popularity as alternative investments. However, they are highly speculative and come with significant price volatility.

Precious Metals:

- Precious metals like gold, silver, platinum, and palladium are often used as a hedge against economic uncertainty and inflation. They can be purchased in physical form or through exchange-traded funds that track the price of the metal.

Collectibles and Alternative Investments:

- Collectibles such as art, rare coins, and vintage cars can be considered alternative investments. These assets can appreciate in value over time but come with unique challenges like illiquidity and difficulty in valuing.

401(k) and Individual Retirement Accounts (IRAs):

- 401(k)s and IRAs are retirement accounts that offer tax advantages. Contributions to these accounts can be invested in various assets, including stocks, bonds, and mutual funds. They are designed to help individuals save for retirement.

Annuities:

- Annuities are insurance products that provide a series of payments to the investor over time, often in retirement. They offer guaranteed income but can be complex and come with fees.

Hedge Funds:

- Hedge funds are investment funds that pool money from accredited investors to employ various strategies, including long-short positions and derivatives trading. Hedge funds aim for higher returns but often require higher minimum investments and have limited transparency.

Private Equity:

- Private equity involves investing in privately-held companies that are not publicly traded. Private equity funds pool money from investors to acquire, manage, and potentially sell companies. This investment class offers the potential for high returns but is illiquid and involves a longer investment horizon.

Understanding Risk and Return:

- Each investment vehicle comes with its own risk and return profile. Generally, higher returns are associated with higher risk. It's crucial to assess your risk tolerance, financial goals, and time horizon when choosing investments.

Diversification:

- Diversification involves spreading investments across different asset classes to reduce risk. A well-diversified portfolio may include a mix of stocks, bonds, real estate, and other assets to mitigate the impact of poor performance in any one area.

Research and Due Diligence:

- Before investing, conduct thorough research and due diligence.

Understand the investment's historical performance, fees, management, and potential risks. Consider consulting financial advisors or professionals if needed.

Aligning Investments with Goals:

- Different investment vehicles serve different purposes. Align your investment choices with your financial goals. For long-term goals like retirement, you might opt for growth-oriented investments, while short-term goals may require more conservative options.

Long-Term Perspective:

- Investing is a long-term endeavor. The compounding effect and the ability to weather market fluctuations are better realized over time. Avoid making impulsive decisions based on short-term market movements.

Regular Portfolio Review:

- Regularly review your investment portfolio to ensure it remains aligned with your goals and risk tolerance. Adjustments may be necessary as your financial situation and market conditions change.

Seeking Professional Advice:

- Investment decisions can be complex. If you're uncertain or lack expertise, consider seeking advice from financial advisors who can help create a tailored investment strategy based on your unique circumstances.

Understanding the different investment vehicles available empowers you to make well-informed decisions that align with your financial aspirations and risk tolerance. By diversifying your portfolio, conducting thorough research, and seeking professional guidance, you can create a balanced investment strategy that works toward achieving your long-term financial goals.

Developing a Balanced Investment Portfolio

Building a balanced investment portfolio is a fundamental aspect of achieving long-term financial success. A well-constructed portfolio combines various asset classes and investment vehicles to manage risk, enhance potential returns, and align with your financial goals and risk tolerance.

Assess Risk Tolerance:

- Before constructing a portfolio, assess your risk tolerance. Understand your comfort level with market fluctuations, potential losses, and investment volatility. Your risk tolerance helps determine the mix of assets in your portfolio.

Set Financial Goals:

- Clarify your financial goals before building your portfolio. Different goals, such as retirement, education, or buying a home, may require varying investment strategies. Define your objectives to guide your asset allocation decisions.

Diversify Across Asset Classes:

- Diversification is a cornerstone of portfolio construction. Allocate your investments across different asset classes, such as stocks, bonds, real estate, and cash. This diversification helps mitigate the impact of poor performance in any single asset.

Understand Correlations:

- Understand how different assets in your portfolio correlate with one another. Assets that move in opposite directions can help balance the portfolio's overall risk. For example, during market downturns, bonds may act as a buffer against stock losses.

Allocate Based on Time Horizon:

- Your investment time horizon influences your asset allocation. Longer time horizons may allow for a higher allocation to growth-oriented assets like stocks, while shorter time horizons might prioritize more conservative investments.

Consider Risk-Return Tradeoff:

- Each asset class offers a unique risk-return tradeoff. Higher-risk assets like stocks generally have the potential for higher returns but come with greater volatility. Assess how much risk you're willing to take for potential returns.

Balancing Growth and Stability:

- A balanced portfolio seeks to achieve both growth and stability. While growth assets can provide long-term returns, stable assets like bonds offer a cushion during market downturns. Finding the right balance is key.

Investment Vehicles:

- Choose investment vehicles that align with your goals and strategy. Consider stocks, bonds, mutual funds, ETFs, and other options based on their risk profiles, fees, and potential returns.

Asset Allocation Strategies:

- Different asset allocation strategies suit different goals. These include aggressive (higher allocation to stocks), conservative (higher allocation to bonds), and balanced (equal mix of stocks and bonds) strategies.

Rebalancing:

- Regularly rebalance your portfolio to maintain your desired asset allocation. Over time, some assets may outperform others, altering the initial balance. Rebalancing ensures you stick to your intended risk level.

Stay Mindful of Fees:

- Fees can erode your investment returns over time. Be aware of management fees, transaction costs, and other charges associated with your investment vehicles. Choose options that align with your budget.

Tax Considerations:

- Understand the tax implications of your investments. Certain assets may generate taxable income or capital gains. Consider tax-efficient strategies like investing in tax-advantaged accounts.

Emergency Fund:

- Before investing, ensure you have an emergency fund. An emergency fund provides a financial safety net and prevents the need to liquidate investments during unexpected expenses.

Long-Term Perspective:

- Successful investing requires a long-term perspective. Short-term market fluctuations are inevitable, but a well-structured portfolio can withstand such volatility and capitalize on long-term growth.

Review and Adjust:

- Regularly review your portfolio's performance and adjust as needed. Life events, market changes, and shifts in your financial goals may necessitate portfolio adjustments.

Professional Advice:

- Seeking advice from financial professionals can provide valuable insights into portfolio construction. Financial advisors can help tailor a strategy that suits your unique circumstances and goals.

Stay Informed:

- Stay updated on market trends, economic developments, and changes in investment vehicles. Informed decision-making enhances your ability to manage your portfolio effectively.

Avoid Emotional Decisions:

- Emotional decisions, such as reacting to market fluctuations, can harm your portfolio's performance. Stick to your long-term strategy and avoid making impulsive choices.

Periodic Reevaluation:

- Life circumstances change, and so should your portfolio. Regularly reevaluate your financial goals, risk tolerance, and investment strategy to ensure your portfolio remains relevant.

Track Performance:

- Monitor the performance of your portfolio against your financial goals. Assess whether your investments are aligning with your objectives and make adjustments as needed.

Stay Adaptable:

- Adaptability is crucial in a changing financial landscape. Be prepared to adjust your portfolio based on evolving market conditions, economic shifts, and personal goals.

Avoid Overconcentration:

- Overconcentration in a single asset or sector increases risk. Diversify to avoid undue exposure to the potential volatility of any one investment.

Stay Patient:

- Investment success requires patience. Avoid chasing short-term gains and remain focused on the long-term growth potential of your diversified portfolio.

Developing a balanced investment portfolio is a dynamic process that requires careful consideration, ongoing review, and alignment with your financial goals. By incorporating diversification, understanding your risk tolerance, and making informed decisions, you can create a portfolio that not only manages risk but also works toward achieving your desired financial outcomes.

Dollar-Cost Averaging vs. Lump-Sum Investing

When it comes to investing, choosing between dollar-cost averaging and lump-sum investing is a decision that can significantly impact your investment strategy. Both approaches have their merits and considerations, and understanding the nuances of each can help you make an informed choice based on your financial goals, risk tolerance, and market outlook.

Dollar-Cost Averaging (DCA):

- DCA involves investing a fixed amount of money at regular intervals, regardless of market conditions. This approach spreads your investments over time and helps mitigate the impact of market volatility.

Advantages of DCA:

- Risk Reduction: DCA minimizes the risk of investing a lump sum just before a market downturn. By investing consistently over time, you're less susceptible to poor market timing.
- Emotional Discipline: DCA encourages disciplined investing, preventing impulsive decisions based on market fluctuations. It helps you stay committed to your investment plan.
- Smoother Entries: DCA allows you to enter the market at various price points, potentially achieving a lower average cost per share.
- Consistency: DCA is suitable for individuals who prefer a steady and consistent investment approach, particularly those with uncertain market outlooks.

Considerations for DCA:

- Opportunity Cost: While DCA reduces the risk of market timing, it also means you might miss out on potential gains if the market performs well during the investment period.

- Longer Time Horizons: DCA works best when you have a longer investment horizon, as it allows for a sufficient number of investment intervals.

Lump-Sum Investing:

- Lump-sum investing involves deploying a large sum of money into the market all at once. This approach provides immediate exposure to market returns but can be riskier if the market declines shortly after investing.

Advantages of Lump-Sum Investing

- Potential for Higher Returns: Lump-sum investing capitalizes on immediate market exposure, potentially leading to higher returns if the market performs well.
- Simplicity: Investing a lump sum simplifies your investment process and requires fewer transactions compared to DCA.
- Time in the Market: The longer your money is in the market, the more it can benefit from compounding returns.

Considerations for Lump-Sum Investing:

- Market Timing Risk: The main drawback of lump-sum investing is the risk of investing just before a market downturn. If the market declines shortly after investing, you could experience immediate losses.
- Emotional Response: Lump-sum investing can trigger emotional responses if the market experiences volatility shortly after investing. Investors might be tempted to make impulsive decisions.
- Short-Term Outlook: Lump-sum investing is more suitable for investors with a positive short-term market outlook who are comfortable with taking on higher immediate risk.

Hybrid Approaches:

- Some investors opt for hybrid approaches that combine both DCA and lump-sum investing. This involves investing a portion of the lump sum immediately and then gradually investing the remaining balance using DCA.

Advantages of Hybrid Approaches:

- Immediate Exposure: The initial lump-sum investment captures immediate market exposure and potential gains.
- Risk Mitigation: Gradually investing the remaining balance using

DCA reduces the risk of poor market timing for the entire sum.

- Emotional Balance: Hybrid approaches offer a balance between immediate exposure and risk reduction, helping investors manage emotional reactions.

Considerations for Hybrid Approaches:

- Complexity: Managing a hybrid approach requires careful planning and execution to ensure that both the lump-sum and DCA components are aligned with your investment strategy.
- Monitoring: Regularly monitor your investments and adjust your hybrid approach as needed based on market conditions and your evolving financial goals.

Personal Factors:

- Your personal financial situation, investment goals, risk tolerance, and market outlook play a significant role in determining whether dollar-cost averaging, lump-sum investing, or a hybrid approach is the right fit for you.

Market Volatility Considerations:

- Market volatility and uncertainty can influence your choice between DCA and lump-sum investing. If the market is particularly turbulent, DCA might provide a more comfortable entry.

Staying the Course:

- Regardless of the approach you choose, the key to successful investing is staying the course. Avoid making impulsive decisions based on short-term market movements and remain focused on your long-term goals.

Professional Guidance:

- If you're uncertain about which approach to take, consider seeking advice from financial professionals. They can help tailor an investment strategy that aligns with your unique circumstances and objectives.

Ultimately, the choice between dollar-cost averaging and lump-sum investing depends on your risk tolerance, investment horizon, market outlook, and emotional disposition. Both approaches have their merits, and understanding how each aligns with your financial goals will help you make a decision that supports your long-term investment success.

Navigating Market Volatility and Risk Management:

Market volatility is an inherent part of investing, and effectively managing risk is essential for achieving long-term financial goals. Navigating market fluctuations requires a combination of prudent strategies, informed decision-making, and a clear understanding of your risk tolerance and investment horizon.

Risk Assessment:

- Begin by assessing your risk tolerance. Understand your comfort level with market ups and downs, as well as the potential for temporary losses. Your risk tolerance serves as a foundation for crafting a risk management strategy that aligns with your emotional disposition and financial objectives.

Diversification:

- Diversifying your investment portfolio is one of the most effective ways to manage risk. By spreading your investments across different asset classes, sectors, and geographic regions, you can reduce the impact of poor performance in any single area. Diversification helps mitigate the risks associated with being overly concentrated in a specific investment.

Asset Allocation:

- Allocate your assets based on your risk tolerance and investment horizon. The right mix of stocks, bonds, and other assets helps strike a balance between potential returns and risk exposure. A well-considered asset allocation takes into account your financial goals, time horizon, and comfort with market volatility.

Emergency Fund:

- Maintaining an emergency fund is essential for risk management. An emergency fund provides a financial safety net that prevents the need to sell investments during unexpected expenses or market downturns. It acts as a buffer, allowing you to weather financial storms without compromising your long-term investments.

Long-Term Perspective:

- Approach investing with a long-term perspective. While short-term market fluctuations are inevitable, they tend to smooth out over time. Staying committed to your investment strategy can help you weather market volatility without making hasty decisions based on short-term events.

Stay Informed:

- Stay updated on market trends, economic indicators, and geopolitical events that can impact the financial markets. Informed decision-making is crucial for effectively navigating market volatility. Regularly consuming reliable financial news and analysis can provide valuable insights.

Avoid Emotional Reactions:

- Emotional reactions to market volatility can lead to poor investment decisions. It's important to avoid making impulsive changes to your portfolio based on short-term market movements driven by fear or greed. Maintain discipline and stick to your long-term strategy.

Systematic Investment:

- Systematic investment, such as dollar-cost averaging (DCA), can help manage market volatility. Regularly investing fixed amounts at predetermined intervals can reduce the impact of market timing. DCA enables you to buy more shares when prices are low and fewer shares when prices are high, effectively averaging out market fluctuations.

Professional Guidance:

- Seeking advice from financial professionals can provide valuable insights during times of market volatility. Financial advisors can help you make informed decisions based on your unique financial situation, risk tolerance, and long-term goals. Their experience and expertise can help you navigate turbulent markets more confidently.

Avoid Timing the Market:

- Timing the market—trying to buy at the bottom and sell at the top—is notoriously challenging. Even seasoned professionals struggle to consistently predict market movements accurately. Attempting to time the market can lead to missed opportunities and heightened risk.

Stay the Course:

- A well-constructed investment plan is built to withstand market volatility. Avoid changing your strategy based on short-term market fluctuations. Staying the course and adhering to your long-term investment plan is often the most prudent approach for achieving your financial objectives.

Review and Adjust:

- Periodically review your investment portfolio and risk management strategy. Adjustments may be necessary as your financial situation, goals, and market conditions change. Regular portfolio reviews help ensure that your investments remain aligned with your evolving objectives.

Portfolio Stress Testing:

- Conduct stress tests on your portfolio to assess its performance under various market scenarios. By simulating different market conditions, you can gain insights into how your investments might behave during times of heightened volatility. This process helps you make informed decisions and refine your risk management strategy.

Hedging Strategies:

- Consider using hedging strategies, such as options or inverse exchange-traded funds (ETFs), to protect your portfolio against market declines. These strategies can help mitigate potential losses during market downturns by providing a counterbalance to your existing investments.

Fixed Income Allocation:

- Allocating a portion of your portfolio to fixed-income assets like bonds can provide stability during market volatility. Bonds typically exhibit lower volatility than stocks and can act as a buffer against market downturns. The income generated from bonds can help offset potential losses in other parts of your portfolio.

Exploring 401(k)s and Their Benefits

A 401(k) retirement savings plan is a valuable tool that offers employees the opportunity to save for their future while benefiting from potential tax advantages and employer contributions. Understanding the ins and outs of 401(k)s and the benefits they provide is essential for securing a comfortable retirement.

Definition and Purpose:

- A 401(k) is a retirement savings plan sponsored by employers that allows employees to contribute a portion of their pre-tax income toward retirement savings. The purpose of a 401(k) is to provide individuals with a tax-efficient way to accumulate funds for their retirement years.

Employee Contributions:

- Employees can contribute a percentage of their salary to their 401(k) on a pre-tax basis. These contributions reduce their taxable income for the year, effectively lowering their overall tax bill. The maximum annual contribution limit is set by the IRS and may vary year to year.

Employer Contributions:

- Many employers offer matching contributions to encourage employees to save for retirement. Employer contributions can be a fixed percentage of the employee's salary or a match based on the employee's contributions, up to a certain limit. This "free money" can significantly boost retirement savings.

Tax Advantages:

- One of the primary benefits of a 401(k) is its tax advantages. Employee contributions are made on a pre-tax basis, meaning they are deducted from the employee's salary before taxes are applied. This lowers the employee's taxable income for the year and results in reduced income tax.

Tax-Deferred Growth:

- Within a 401(k), investments grow tax-deferred. This means that any gains, dividends, or interest earned within the account are not subject to taxes until withdrawals are made during retirement. Tax deferral allows investments to compound more effectively over time.

Variety of Investment Options:

- 401(k)s typically offer a range of investment options, including mutual funds, index funds, target-date funds, and sometimes individual stocks and bonds. This allows participants to create a diversified investment portfolio that aligns with their risk tolerance and financial goals.

Portability:

- 401(k)s are generally portable, meaning that if you change jobs, you can typically roll over your 401(k) funds into a new employer's plan, an Individual Retirement Account (IRA), or another qualified retirement account without incurring taxes or penalties.

Access to Funds:

- While a 401(k) is designed for retirement savings, some plans offer loans or hardship withdrawals under specific circumstances. However, withdrawing funds before age 59½ typically incurs taxes and penalties, eroding the potential benefits of the account.

Contribution Limits:

- The IRS sets annual contribution limits for 401(k)s to ensure that higher-income individuals do not disproportionately benefit. These limits may change over time and are influenced by the individual's age and income level.

Vesting Schedule:

- Vesting refers to an employee's ownership of employer contributions. Some 401(k) plans have a vesting schedule that determines how long an employee must stay with the company before the employer contributions become fully vested. Vesting schedules vary by plan.

Automatic Enrollment:

- Some employers offer automatic enrollment in their 401(k) plans, meaning that eligible employees are automatically enrolled in the plan unless they choose to opt out. This helps boost retirement savings participation rates.

Diversification and Risk Management:

- Through a 401(k), employees have the opportunity to diversify their investments across various asset classes. Diversification helps manage risk and ensures that your retirement savings aren't overly dependent on the performance of a single investment.

Retirement Planning:

- A 401(k) is a cornerstone of retirement planning. Consistently contributing to your 401(k) throughout your career can help you accumulate substantial savings for retirement. It's essential to periodically review and adjust your contributions and investment selections based on your financial goals.

Retirement Match Maximization:

- Taking full advantage of employer matching contributions is a smart strategy. Aim to contribute enough to your 401(k) to receive the maximum employer match—it's essentially free money that can significantly enhance your retirement nest egg.

Compound Growth Potential:

- The combination of pre-tax contributions, tax-deferred growth, and potential employer matching can lead to substantial compound growth over the course of your career. Compound growth is the exponential increase in your savings over time due to reinvested earnings.

Inflation Hedge:

- Retirement planning requires accounting for the impact of inflation on your purchasing power. The compounding effect of a 401(k) helps combat the eroding effects of inflation by growing your investments at a rate that outpaces rising costs.

Reduced Reliance on Social Security:

- A well-funded 401(k) can reduce your reliance on Social Security benefits during retirement. It provides an additional source of income that you control, contributing to your financial independence in retirement.

Understanding Traditional IRAs and Roth IRAs

Individual Retirement Accounts (IRAs) are popular retirement savings vehicles that offer tax advantages to help individuals build a financially secure retirement. Two common types of IRAs are Traditional IRAs and Roth IRAs. Each type has its own set of rules, benefits, and considerations, making it important to understand their nuances to make informed decisions about your retirement planning.

Traditional IRAs:

- **Tax Deductible Contributions:** Contributions to a Traditional IRA may be tax-deductible, which means they can reduce your taxable income for the year in which you make the contribution. This can result in immediate tax savings, potentially lowering your overall tax bill.
- **Tax-Deferred Growth:** Within a Traditional IRA, your investments grow tax-deferred. This means that any gains, dividends, or interest earned within the account are not subject to taxes until you make withdrawals during retirement. Tax deferral allows your investments to compound more effectively over time.
- **Required Minimum Distributions (RMDs):** Traditional IRAs have a requirement that you start taking withdrawals—known as Required Minimum Distributions (RMDs)—by age 72. RMDs are calculated based on your age and the balance in your account, ensuring that you gradually distribute your retirement savings.
- **Tax Treatment of Withdrawals:** When you withdraw funds from a Traditional IRA during retirement, those withdrawals are treated as ordinary income and are subject to income tax. The idea is that you'll likely be in a lower tax bracket during retirement, potentially resulting in lower tax liability.
- **Early Withdrawal Penalties:** If you withdraw funds from a

Traditional IRA before age 59½, you'll generally face a 10% penalty in addition to income tax on the withdrawn amount. Some exceptions, such as using the funds for qualified education expenses or a first-time home purchase, may waive the penalty.

Roth IRAs:

- **Tax-Free Qualified Withdrawals:** Roth IRAs offer tax-free withdrawals on qualified distributions. This means that if you follow the rules, you won't owe any income tax on the withdrawals you make during retirement. This can be a significant advantage, especially if your investments have grown substantially.
- **Contributions Aren't Tax-Deductible:** Unlike Traditional IRAs, contributions to Roth IRAs are made with after-tax dollars, meaning they don't provide an immediate tax deduction. However, this also means that your withdrawals, including the earnings, can be tax-free during retirement.
- **No RMDs:** Roth IRAs do not have required minimum distributions (RMDs) during your lifetime. This allows you to keep your funds invested and potentially continue growing them, providing more flexibility in your retirement income planning.
- **Early Withdrawal Flexibility:** You can withdraw your Roth IRA contributions (but not earnings) at any time without facing taxes or penalties. This provides more flexibility in case you need to access your savings before retirement.
- **Qualified Distributions Criteria:** To make tax-free withdrawals from a Roth IRA, your distributions must be "qualified." Generally, this means you need to be at least 59½ years old and have had the Roth IRA open for at least five years.

Choosing Between Traditional and Roth IRAs:

- **Tax Considerations:** The decision between Traditional and Roth IRAs often comes down to your current and anticipated future tax situation. If you expect your tax rate to be lower during retirement, a Traditional IRA's immediate tax deduction might be more beneficial. On the other hand, if you anticipate being in a higher tax bracket during retirement, a Roth IRA's tax-free withdrawals could be advantageous.

- **Retirement Horizon:** Consider your age and time until retirement. If you have many years until retirement, a Roth IRA's tax-free growth potential can be advantageous. If retirement is closer, a Traditional IRA's upfront tax deduction might have a more immediate impact.
- **Current Tax Bracket:** Your current tax bracket also plays a role. If you're currently in a high tax bracket, contributing to a Traditional IRA can provide significant tax savings now. If you're in a lower tax bracket, a Roth IRA's long-term tax-free withdrawals might be more appealing.
- **Diversification:** Some individuals choose to diversify their retirement savings by contributing to both Traditional and Roth IRAs. This way, you have a mix of tax-deferred and tax-free options, which can offer greater flexibility during retirement.

Conversion Strategies:

- **Roth Conversion:** If you have a Traditional IRA, you can convert it to a Roth IRA through a process known as a Roth conversion. This involves paying taxes on the converted amount in the year of conversion but can provide tax-free growth and withdrawals in the future.

Contribution Limits and Eligibility

- **Contribution Limits:** Both Traditional and Roth IRAs have contribution limits set by the IRS. These limits may change annually and can vary based on your age and income.
- **Income Limits:** While anyone with earned income can contribute to a Traditional IRA, income limits exist for Roth IRAs. If your income exceeds a certain threshold, you may not be eligible to contribute directly to a Roth IRA. However, Roth conversions are available to high-income individuals.

Contribution Limits and Tax Implications:

When it comes to retirement savings accounts like 401(k)s, Traditional IRAs, and Roth IRAs, understanding contribution limits and tax implications is crucial. These limits dictate how much you can contribute to these accounts each year, and the tax implications determine how your contributions impact your current and future tax liabilities. Let's delve into these important aspects of retirement planning:

Contribution Limits:

- **401(k) Contribution Limits:** The IRS sets annual contribution limits for 401(k) plans. As of [current year], the maximum contribution limit for employees under the age of 50 is [$19,500]. Employees aged 50 and older can make catch-up contributions, with an additional [$6,500] allowed, bringing their total limit to [$26,000]. These limits may change in subsequent years due to inflation adjustments.
- **Traditional and Roth IRA Contribution Limits:** For Traditional and Roth IRAs, the annual contribution limits for individuals under the age of 50 is [$6,000] as of [current year]. Those aged 50 and older can contribute an extra [$1,000] as a catch-up contribution, resulting in a total limit of [$7,000]. These limits may also be adjusted for

inflation in the future.

Tax Implications:

- **Pre-Tax Contributions:** Contributions to 401(k)s and Traditional IRAs are typically made on a pre-tax basis. This means that the amount you contribute reduces your taxable income for the current year. You won't pay income tax on these contributions until you withdraw the funds during retirement.
- **Tax-Deferred Growth:** Both 401(k)s and Traditional IRAs offer tax-deferred growth. The earnings, dividends, and interest generated within these accounts are not taxed until withdrawal. This allows your investments to compound over time without the drag of annual taxes.
- **Tax-Free Qualified Withdrawals (Roth IRAs):** Roth IRAs offer a different tax structure. Contributions to Roth IRAs are made with after-tax dollars, so they don't provide an immediate tax deduction. However, qualified withdrawals from Roth IRAs, including earnings, are entirely tax-free during retirement.
- **Tax Treatment of Withdrawals (Traditional IRAs and 401(k)s):** Withdrawals from Traditional IRAs and 401(k)s during retirement are treated as ordinary income and are subject to income tax. This means you'll owe taxes on the amount you withdraw, which can impact your overall retirement income strategy.
- **Early Withdrawal Penalties:** Withdrawing funds from a 401(k) or Traditional IRA before age 59½ may result in a 10% early withdrawal penalty, in addition to the regular income tax. Some exceptions, like using the funds for qualified education or a first-time home purchase, may waive the penalty.
- **Required Minimum Distributions (Traditional IRAs and 401(k)s):** Traditional IRAs and 401(k)s have required minimum distributions (RMDs) starting at age 72. These distributions ensure that you begin withdrawing funds from your tax-deferred accounts, which in turn generates taxable income.

- **No RMDs for Roth IRAs:** Roth IRAs don't have RMDs during your lifetime. This means you can let your investments grow tax-free for as long as you wish, giving you greater control over when and how you access your retirement savings.

Choosing the Right Strategy:

- **Tax Considerations:** When choosing between pre-tax contributions (Traditional) and after-tax contributions (Roth), consider your current and expected future tax rates. If you believe your tax rate will be lower in retirement, a Traditional IRA or 401(k) might be advantageous. If you anticipate a higher tax rate during retirement, a Roth option could be more suitable.
- **Diversification:** Some individuals choose a combination of accounts to diversify their tax exposure. For example, contributing to a 401(k) to maximize employer matching and then contributing to a Roth IRA for tax-free withdrawals can offer a balanced approach.

Strategic Planning:

- **Contribution Timing:** Maximize your contributions early in the year to take full advantage of potential investment growth. For example, if you have the means, contribute to your retirement accounts at the beginning of the year rather than waiting until the deadline.
- **Employer Matching:** If your employer offers a 401(k) matching contribution, aim to contribute enough to receive the full match. Employer matches are essentially free money that can significantly enhance your retirement savings.
- **Tax Planning:** Coordinate your retirement contributions with your overall tax planning strategy. Consider consulting with a financial advisor or tax professional to ensure your retirement savings align with your broader financial goals.

Strategies for Optimizing Retirement Account Contributions

Effectively optimizing your retirement account contributions can significantly impact your financial security during retirement. By strategically managing contributions to accounts like 401(k)s, Traditional IRAs, and Roth IRAs, you can maximize tax benefits, take advantage of employer matches, and harness the power of compound growth. Here are key strategies to consider:

1. Start Early:

- The power of compounding works best over time. The earlier you begin contributing to retirement accounts, the more time your investments have to grow. Even small contributions made consistently can accumulate into substantial savings due to compound interest.

2. Maximize Employer Matches:

- If your employer offers a 401(k) match, strive to contribute enough to receive the full match. This is essentially free money that significantly boosts your retirement savings. Failing to take advantage of an employer match is like leaving money on the table.

3. Contribute Tax-Efficiently:

- Depending on your tax situation, consider the benefits of pre-tax (Traditional) and after-tax (Roth) contributions. Pre-tax contributions reduce your taxable income for the current year, while Roth contributions allow for tax-free withdrawals during retirement. Balancing both can provide tax diversification in retirement.

4. Dollar-Cost Averaging:

- Contribute consistently over time using dollar-cost averaging. Regular contributions spread out over the course of the year can help mitigate the impact of market volatility and reduce the risk of making large contributions during market peaks.

5. Prioritize Maxing Out:

- Aim to contribute the maximum allowed amount to your retirement accounts. For instance, contribute up to the annual limit of your 401(k) and IRA. Maxing out these accounts maximizes your tax advantages and accelerates your retirement savings growth.

6. Utilize Catch-Up Contributions:

- If you're age 50 or older, take advantage of catch-up contributions allowed by the IRS. For 401(k)s and Traditional IRAs, this allows additional contributions beyond the standard limit. This can make a significant difference in your retirement savings in the years leading up to retirement.

7. Tax Refund Strategy:

- If you receive a tax refund, consider allocating a portion of it to your retirement accounts. This can be a smart way to boost your contributions without impacting your current cash flow.

8. Bonuses and Windfalls:

- Use unexpected financial windfalls, such as work bonuses or tax refunds, to make lump-sum contributions to your retirement accounts. These contributions can have an immediate impact on your retirement savings.

9. Consistently Increase Contributions:

- Commit to increasing your contributions annually or whenever you receive a salary increase. This helps ensure that your retirement savings keep pace with inflation and your changing financial situation.

10. Budget Adjustments:

- Analyze your budget for areas where you can cut back on discretionary spending. Redirect the money saved into your retirement accounts. Sacrificing short-term wants for long-term financial security can be a rewarding trade-off.

11. Roth Conversion Strategy:

- If you're in a lower income tax bracket for a particular year, consider converting some or all of your Traditional IRA funds to a Roth IRA. This strategy allows you to pay taxes at a lower rate and benefit from tax-free growth in the Roth IRA.

12. Assess Retirement Goals:

- Regularly evaluate your retirement goals, lifestyle expectations, and expected expenses. Adjust your contribution strategy accordingly to ensure you're on track to meet your retirement needs.

13. Professional Guidance:

- Consult with a financial advisor to develop a personalized retirement contribution strategy. A professional can help you optimize your contributions based on your unique financial situation, goals, and risk tolerance.

14. Automated Contributions:

- Set up automatic contributions to your retirement accounts with each paycheck. This eliminates the need for manual transfers, ensures consistency, and reduces the temptation to spend the money elsewhere.

15. Periodic Reviews:

- Review your retirement contribution strategy annually or whenever significant life changes occur. Adjustments may be necessary based on factors such as income changes, tax law updates, and market performance.

Optimizing retirement account contributions requires a well-informed approach that considers your financial situation, goals, and tax outlook. By implementing these strategies and remaining disciplined in your approach, you can build a strong foundation for a financially secure retirement.

Rollovers and Transfers: Managing Retirement Accounts Effectively

Managing retirement accounts effectively is an essential aspect of financial planning, and understanding how to handle rollovers and transfers is a crucial component of that. Rollovers and transfers allow you to move funds between different retirement accounts while maintaining tax advantages and avoiding unnecessary penalties. This strategic approach can help you optimize your retirement savings and streamline your financial strategy. Let's delve into the intricacies of rollovers and transfers:

Understanding Rollovers and Transfers:

- **Rollover:** A rollover involves moving funds from one retirement account to another of the same type. For example, you might move funds from one 401(k) to another 401(k) or from one Traditional IRA to another Traditional IRA.
- **Transfer:** A transfer refers to moving funds directly between accounts of the same type. This often happens between financial institutions and ensures that the funds move seamlessly without the account holder ever handling the money.

Reasons for Rollovers and Transfers:

- **Changing Jobs:** When you change jobs, you might need to decide what to do with your old employer-sponsored retirement account, such as a 401(k). You can choose to roll it over into your new employer's plan or into an IRA.
- **Consolidation:** You might have multiple retirement accounts from different employers or financial institutions. Rollovers and transfers allow you to consolidate these accounts, making it easier to manage your investments and track your progress.
- **Better Investment Options:** If your existing retirement account lacks the investment options you desire, you can roll over or transfer

your funds to a new account that provides better investment choices.

- **Retirement Planning:** As you approach retirement, you might decide to consolidate your retirement accounts to simplify distributions and better manage your retirement income strategy.
- **Avoiding Penalties:** Properly executed rollovers and transfers can help you avoid penalties and taxes that can occur if you were to withdraw funds from a retirement account and not reinvest them within the specified time frame.

Types of Rollovers:

- **Direct Rollover:** In a direct rollover, funds are transferred directly from one retirement account to another. You don't touch the money, and this helps avoid any tax implications or penalties.
- **Indirect Rollover:** With an indirect rollover, you receive the funds from one account and have 60 days to deposit them into another eligible retirement account. However, this comes with risks, including the potential for taxes and penalties if the process isn't completed correctly.

Guidelines for Successful Rollovers and Transfers:

- **Maintain Timeline:** If you opt for an indirect rollover, ensure you complete the process within the 60-day window to avoid taxes and penalties.
- **Follow Tax Rules:** Different retirement accounts have different tax rules. For instance, Roth IRAs cannot be rolled over into Traditional IRAs without facing tax consequences. Understanding the tax implications is crucial.
- **Choose Direct Rollovers:** Whenever possible, choose direct rollovers. They're simpler, safer, and eliminate the risk of mishandling the funds, which could result in taxes and penalties.

Steps for a Smooth Rollover or Transfer:

1. **Select New Account:** Choose the new retirement account where you want to move your funds. This could be a new employer's plan, an IRA, or another eligible account.
2. **Contact Financial Institutions:** Reach out to both the old and new financial institutions to initiate the rollover or transfer process. They will guide you through the necessary steps and paperwork.
3. **Complete Necessary Paperwork:** Fill out any required forms, provide necessary documentation, and ensure that both institutions are aware of your intent.
4. **Initiate the Transfer:** If you're transferring directly, the financial institutions will handle the process seamlessly. If you're conducting an indirect rollover, ensure you receive the funds within the specified timeframe.
5. **Deposit Funds:** If you're conducting an indirect rollover, deposit the funds into the new account within 60 days. Be cautious of the one-rollover-per-year rule, which limits you to one indirect rollover within a 12-month period.
6. **Keep Records:** Maintain records of the transaction, including forms, correspondence, and deposit receipts. This documentation can be useful for tax reporting and verification.

Considerations and Precautions:

- **Tax Withholding:** If you're conducting an indirect rollover, your old retirement account may withhold 20% of the funds for taxes. To avoid penalties, you must replenish this amount when depositing the funds into the new account.
- **Professional Guidance:** If you're unsure about the process or tax implications, consider consulting a financial advisor or tax professional. They can help you navigate the complexities and make informed decisions.

Assessing Your Debt Load and Interest Rates

Managing your debt effectively is a crucial step toward achieving financial independence. By understanding how to evaluate your debt load and navigate interest rates, you can make informed decisions that lead to improved financial health. Here's a closer look at the key considerations:

Debt Assessment:

- **Debt-to-Income Ratio:** One of the initial steps is to calculate your debt-to-income ratio. This ratio reflects the portion of your income that goes toward debt payments. A lower ratio generally indicates better financial stability.

Debt Overview:

- **List and Categorization:** Begin by creating a comprehensive list of all your debts. Categorize them based on the type of debt—credit cards, loans, mortgages, and any other financial obligations.

Interest Rate Understanding:

- **Variable vs. Fixed Rates:** Different debts come with different types of interest rates. Understand whether your rates are fixed (unchanging) or variable (changing based on market conditions).

Importance of Interest Rates:

- **Impact on Payments:** Interest rates directly affect the total amount you pay over time. Higher rates result in more interest paid, increasing the cost of your debt.
- **Prioritization:** When paying down debt, prioritize debts with higher interest rates. These tend to accumulate more interest over time, becoming costlier in the long run.

Credit Card Debt:

- **High-Interest Nature:** Credit cards often have higher interest rates compared to other types of debt. Paying off credit card balances promptly can save you substantial money.

Mortgages and Loans:

- **Long-Term Impact:** Mortgages and loans may have lower interest rates but longer terms. Although the rates are lower, the extended period means more interest paid over time.

Student Loans:

- **Types of Loans:** Student loans can have varying interest rates based on federal or private sources. Federal loans may offer more flexible repayment options.

Personal Loans:

- **Variability:** Interest rates for personal loans can vary widely based on factors like your credit score and the lender. Shop around for the best rates.

Consolidation and Refinancing:

- **Debt Consolidation Loans:** Consider consolidating multiple debts into one loan with a lower interest rate. This simplifies payments and may save money.
- **Mortgage Refinancing:** Refinancing a mortgage to a lower interest rate can reduce monthly payments and save money over the loan's term.
- **Student Loan Refinancing:** Similar to mortgages, refinancing student loans can lead to lower interest rates and more manageable payments.

Credit Score Impact:

- **Interest Rate and Credit Score:** Your credit score plays a significant role in determining the interest rates you're offered. A higher credit score often translates to lower rates.

Payoff Strategies:

- **Debt Avalanche:** Prioritize paying off debts with the highest interest rates first. This approach minimizes the overall interest paid.
- **Debt Snowball:** Focus on paying off smaller debts first to build momentum and motivation. This strategy may not save as much on interest but offers psychological benefits.

Negotiating Interest Rates:

- **Credit Card Companies:** In some cases, credit card companies may be open to negotiating interest rates, especially if you have a good payment history.
- **Lenders and Servicers:** For loans, explore options to negotiate interest rates directly with lenders or loan servicers.

Creating a Debt Repayment Plan

Embarking on a journey toward financial independence requires a well-structured debt repayment plan. This comprehensive approach empowers you to regain financial control, minimize interest costs, and work steadfastly toward a debt-free future. In the pursuit of crafting an effective debt repayment plan, consider these essential aspects:

Assess Your Debts:

- **List All Debts:** Begin your debt repayment journey by meticulously listing all your debts, encompassing credit cards, loans, and any other financial obligations. This comprehensive overview serves as the cornerstone of your repayment strategy.
- **Interest Rates:** Delve into the specifics of each debt by documenting their associated interest rates. This knowledge empowers you to prioritize paying off debts with higher interest rates, ultimately saving you more money over time.
- **Minimum Payments:** Understand the baseline by recording the minimum monthly payments required for each debt. Ensuring you meet these minimums maintains your financial stability and avoids penalties.

Determine Your Budget:

- **Evaluate Income and Expenses:** Thoroughly assess your monthly income and expenses to gauge the extent of your discretionary income available for debt repayment.
- **Trim Unnecessary Spending:** Exercise a critical eye to identify areas within your budget where you can strategically cut back on discretionary spending. By reallocating these funds toward debt repayment, you can substantially expedite your progress.

Select a Repayment Strategy:

- **Debt Snowball:** Embark on your debt repayment journey by prioritizing the smallest debt first, while concurrently making minimum payments on your other debts. As each debt is paid off, redirect the freed-up funds toward the next smallest debt. This approach offers psychological victories along the way, boosting motivation.
- **Debt Avalanche:** Alternatively, focus your efforts on eliminating debts with the highest interest rates. This method—often likened to an "avalanche" of debt reduction—mathematically minimizes the total interest paid over time.
- **Custom Approach:** Recognize that individual financial circumstances vary. Tailor your repayment strategy to align with your preferences, goals, and unique financial situation. You might choose to merge elements of the snowball and avalanche methods to create a hybrid approach that suits your needs.

Set Specific Goals:

- **SMART Goals:** Transform your aspirations into SMART goals—ones that are Specific, Measurable, Achievable, Relevant, and Time-bound. For instance, aim to eliminate $5,000 in credit card debt within a specific time frame of 12 months.
- **Visualize Success:** Harness the power of visualization by creating tangible representations of your goals, such as a debt payoff chart. Visual cues act as motivational reminders of your progress and the achievements you're working toward.

Prioritize and Allocate Funds:

- **Allocating Extra Funds:** Capitalize on opportunities to expedite your debt repayment by designating any additional funds toward this endeavor. Windfalls, tax refunds, or bonuses can significantly bolster your progress.
- **Minimum Payments:** While concentrating on paying off specific

debts, remember to consistently fulfill minimum payments on all your obligations. This practice safeguards you from penalties and potential setbacks.

Negotiate Interest Rates and Terms:

- **Contact Lenders:** Explore the possibility of negotiating with your creditors to secure lower interest rates or more favorable repayment terms. Demonstrating your commitment to repayment might open the door to beneficial arrangements.

Monitor and Adjust:

- **Regular Tracking:** Continuously monitor your progress as you navigate your debt repayment plan. Regularly reviewing your accomplishments motivates you to stay on course.
- **Adapt to Changes:** Be adaptable in adjusting your strategy if unexpected financial changes occur. Flexibility ensures your plan remains aligned with your evolving circumstances.

Celebrate Achievements:

- **Milestones Matter:** Celebrate each milestone along your debt repayment journey. Recognize your achievements and use them as stepping stones toward your ultimate goal of financial independence.

Creating a debt repayment plan isn't just about eliminating debt—it's about regaining control of your financial narrative, investing in your future, and cultivating sound financial habits that will serve you well beyond your debt-free journey. Your proactive approach to managing debt is a testament to your commitment to shaping a financially secure and empowered future.

The Snowball vs. Avalanche Method

When it comes to conquering debt, having a clear strategy can make all the difference. Two widely recognized methods, the snowball and avalanche approaches, offer distinct paths to debt repayment. By understanding the intricacies of each method, you can make an informed decision that aligns with your financial goals and circumstances. Let's delve into the finer details of the snowball and avalanche methods:

The Snowball Method:

- **Overview:** Developed by personal finance expert Dave Ramsey, the snowball method is designed to build motivation and momentum by targeting smaller debts first.
- **Execution:** Begin by compiling a list of your debts, arranging them from the smallest balance to the largest, regardless of interest rates.
- **Payment Focus:** Allocate extra funds toward the debt with the smallest balance, while maintaining minimum payments on other debts.
- **Psychological Boost:** As smaller debts are eliminated, you experience a psychological victory, bolstering your commitment to the debt repayment journey.
- **Advantages:** The snowball method leverages psychological wins to fuel motivation, making it particularly effective for individuals who thrive on visible progress.

The Avalanche Method:

- **Overview:** The avalanche method prioritizes minimizing interest payments by concentrating on debts with the highest interest rates.
- **Execution:** Create a list of debts ordered by interest rates, from the highest to the lowest.
- **Payment Focus:** Channel additional funds toward the debt carrying the highest interest rate, while making minimum payments on other

debts.

- **Interest Savings:** The avalanche method minimizes the total interest paid over time, making it a financially efficient approach.
- **Advantages:** By saving on interest costs, the avalanche method accelerates the path to debt freedom and reduces the overall financial burden.

Choosing Between the Two:

- **Psychological vs. Financial Consideration:** While the snowball method offers emotional satisfaction through quick wins, the avalanche method optimizes long-term financial outcomes.
- **Personal Preferences:** Reflect on your individual preferences and what drives you. If the satisfaction of marking off small victories is essential, the snowball method might be your choice. If saving on interest costs is your primary focus, the avalanche method could be more appealing.
- **Long-Term Impact:** While the snowball method might lead to more interest paid in the long run, the disparity might not be substantial enough to offset the motivational benefits it provides.
- **Hybrid Approach:** Tailor a hybrid strategy that combines aspects of both methods. Begin with the snowball method for immediate progress and then transition to the avalanche approach as your enthusiasm and determination grow.

Factors to Consider:

- **Interest Rate Differences:** Evaluate the difference in interest rates between your smallest debt and your highest interest rate debt. If the gap is minimal, the psychological boost of the snowball method might outweigh the interest savings of the avalanche approach.
- **Alignment with Goals:** Ensure your chosen method aligns with your overarching financial objectives. Whether you're aiming for rapid debt elimination or minimizing interest expenditure, your chosen

method should resonate with your goals.

Consolidation and Refinancing Options

When managing multiple debts becomes overwhelming, consolidation and refinancing options can provide relief by simplifying your financial landscape and potentially reducing interest rates. These strategies involve restructuring your debts to make them more manageable and cost-effective. Let's delve deeper into the consolidation and refinancing options available to help you regain control of your financial journey:

Debt Consolidation:

- **Combining Multiple Debts:** Debt consolidation involves merging multiple debts into a single, more manageable payment. This can streamline your financial obligations, making them easier to track and reducing the risk of missing payments.
- **Methods of Consolidation:** There are various methods to consolidate debts, including personal loans, balance transfer credit cards, and debt consolidation loans.
- **Pros and Cons:** While consolidation simplifies your payments, it's essential to carefully consider the terms, fees, and interest rates associated with the new consolidation method. It's not a one-size-fits-all solution, and understanding the implications is crucial.

Benefits of Debt Consolidation:

- **Simplified Payments:** Managing a single payment is less complex and reduces the chances of overlooking due dates.
- **Potentially Lower Interest:** If your consolidation method offers a lower interest rate, you could save money over time.
- **Improved Credit Score:** Timely payments on a consolidation loan can positively impact your credit score.

Drawbacks of Debt Consolidation:

- **Extended Repayment Period:** Some consolidation methods might extend your repayment period, meaning you'll be in debt for a more extended period.
- **Origination Fees:** Certain consolidation options might come with origination fees or other charges, which could offset potential savings.

Mortgage Refinancing:

- **Refinancing Your Mortgage:** Mortgage refinancing involves replacing your existing mortgage with a new one that offers better terms, such as a lower interest rate or different repayment structure.
- **Cash-Out Refinancing:** This option allows you to borrow additional funds against your home's equity while refinancing. It can be used for debt consolidation, home improvements, or other financial needs.
- **Considerations:** Mortgage refinancing typically requires closing costs and a thorough evaluation of the potential savings versus the costs involved.

Student Loan Refinancing:

- **Interest Rate Reduction:** Student loan refinancing involves replacing existing student loans with a new loan that offers a lower interest rate.
- **Private vs. Federal Loans:** While refinancing can lower interest rates, it may result in the loss of federal loan benefits such as income-driven repayment plans and loan forgiveness options.
- **Eligibility:** Qualifying for student loan refinancing often requires a strong credit history and financial stability.

Auto Loan Refinancing:

- **Lower Interest Rates:** Refinancing an auto loan aims to secure a lower interest rate, which can reduce the total cost of the loan.
- **Savings Potential:** If your credit score has improved since you

initially took out the auto loan, refinancing can lead to significant savings.

- **Loan Terms:** Some lenders may offer extended loan terms, which can reduce your monthly payments but potentially extend the overall repayment period.

Home Equity Loans and Lines of Credit:

- **Using Home Equity:** A home equity loan or line of credit allows you to borrow against the equity in your home.
- **Interest Rates:** These options often have lower interest rates compared to other forms of borrowing.
- **Risk Considerations:** Borrowing against your home carries the risk of losing your property if you're unable to make payments.

Balancing Debt Repayment with Savings and Investments

Striking the right balance between debt repayment, savings, and investments is a critical aspect of achieving financial independence. While it's essential to pay off debts efficiently, neglecting savings and investments can hinder your overall financial progress. Here's a comprehensive look at how to navigate this delicate equilibrium:

Prioritizing Debt Repayment:

- **High-Interest Debts:** Begin by prioritizing high-interest debts, such as credit card balances. These debts accrue substantial interest over time and can impede your financial growth.
- **Snowball or Avalanche:** Choose a debt repayment strategy that suits your financial personality. The snowball method offers quick wins, while the avalanche method minimizes interest costs.
- **Emergency Fund:** Before aggressively paying off debt, establish a small emergency fund to cover unforeseen expenses. This prevents you from accumulating more high-interest debt in emergencies.

Building an Emergency Fund:

- **Safety Net:** An emergency fund provides a financial cushion, reducing the need to rely on credit cards or loans during unexpected situations.
- **Three to Six Months:** Aim to save three to six months' worth of living expenses in your emergency fund. This amount can cover essential costs during job loss or medical emergencies.

Starting with Small Investments:

- **Simultaneous Saving:** While repaying debts, start making small contributions to your savings and investment accounts. Consistency is key, even if the amounts are modest.

- **Employer Matching:** If your employer offers a retirement plan with a match, contribute enough to maximize their match. This is essentially free money toward your future.

Benefits of Simultaneous Saving and Investing:

- **Compound Interest:** The earlier you start investing, the more time your investments have to benefit from compound interest, which amplifies your returns over time.
- **Financial Security:** Building savings and investments simultaneously establishes a foundation of financial security and prepares you for various life stages.

Long-Term Debt and Investment Considerations:

- **Mortgage Debt:** While focusing on high-interest debt, consider the benefits of keeping low-interest mortgage debt. Investing may yield higher returns than paying off low-interest debt.
- **Student Loans:** Evaluate your student loan interest rates and whether your investments can potentially outpace these rates over time.

Creating a Balance:

- **Allocating Funds:** Allocate a portion of your budget to both debt repayment and savings/investments. This balanced approach prevents neglecting either aspect.
- **Review and Adjust:** Periodically reassess your financial situation and adjust your allocations as your circumstances evolve.

When to Shift Focus:

- **Lower Interest Debts:** As high-interest debts are paid off, shift your focus to moderate-interest debts. The urgency to pay off lower-interest debts may decrease.

- **Maximizing Investments:** Once high-interest debts are cleared, allocate more funds to investments, taking advantage of compounding growth.

Final Considerations:

- **Customization:** Every individual's financial journey is unique. Customize your approach based on your debt levels, interest rates, investment opportunities, and overall goals.
- **Professional Guidance:** Consider seeking advice from financial advisors or experts who can offer personalized insights tailored to your situation.

Balancing debt repayment with savings and investments requires careful planning and continuous adjustments. By prioritizing both debt reduction and future financial growth, you're building a solid foundation for your journey toward financial independence.

Identifying Marketable Skills and Talents

Discovering and harnessing your marketable skills and talents is a pivotal step towards achieving financial independence. These unique abilities can open doors to various income-generating opportunities and help you carve a successful path in the ever-evolving job market. Here's an in-depth exploration of how to identify and leverage your marketable skills and talents:

Self-Reflection:

- **Skills Inventory:** Conduct a comprehensive inventory of your skills, both hard and soft. Hard skills encompass technical expertise, while soft skills include communication, leadership, and problem-solving.
- **Passions and Interests:** Reflect on your hobbies and interests. Sometimes, your hobbies can be turned into lucrative ventures with the right approach.

Personal and Professional Experiences:

- **Work Experience:** Evaluate your work history for skills gained through various roles and responsibilities.
- **Educational Background:** Consider the knowledge and skills acquired during your education, both formal and informal.
- **Volunteer Activities:** Skills acquired through volunteering can be just as valuable as those gained in a professional setting.

Seek Feedback:

- **Ask Peers:** Seek feedback from colleagues, friends, and mentors. They may identify skills and talents you may not recognize in yourself.
- **Strengths Assessment:** Consider taking strengths assessments or personality tests to gain insights into your unique strengths.

Cross-Reference with Market Demand:

- **Research Job Trends:** Investigate current job trends and industries with high demand for specific skills. This can guide your skill development efforts.
- **Online Platforms:** Browse online job boards and freelance platforms to see what skills are in demand and what opportunities are available.

Leveraging Marketable Skills:

- **Freelancing:** Offer your skills as a freelancer in areas such as writing, graphic design, programming, or digital marketing.
- **Consulting:** Leverage your expertise to offer consulting services to individuals or businesses in your field.
- **Entrepreneurship:** Transform your skills into a business idea. This could involve creating products, offering services, or starting an online business.

Investing in Skill Development:

- **Continuous Learning:** Commit to lifelong learning to enhance and expand your skillset. Online courses, workshops, and certifications can help you stay competitive.
- **Networking:** Attend industry events, workshops, and conferences to network with professionals and gain insights into emerging trends.

Personal Branding:

- **Online Presence:** Create a strong online presence through a personal website, social media, and professional networking sites like LinkedIn.
- **Showcase Portfolio:** Display your work or projects to demonstrate your skills and talents to potential clients or employers.

Adaptability and Evolution:

- **Embrace Change:** The job market evolves rapidly. Be open to adapting your skills and learning new ones to stay relevant.
- **Multiple Streams:** Develop a diverse skillset to have multiple income streams and the ability to pivot if needed.

Final Considerations:

- **Passion and Profit:** Strive to align your marketable skills and talents with your passions. This connection can lead to more fulfilling and sustainable income sources.
- **Patience and Persistence:** Building a successful career based on your skills and talents takes time and effort. Stay patient and persistent in your pursuit.

Identifying your marketable skills and talents is a powerful tool in your journey towards financial independence. By leveraging what makes you unique, you can create opportunities that not only provide income but also bring you fulfillment and satisfaction.

Navigating the Gig Economy and Freelancing

The gig economy and freelancing have revolutionized the way people work, offering flexibility, autonomy, and diverse income opportunities. Navigating this dynamic landscape requires a strategic approach to secure consistent work, manage finances, and thrive in this ever-evolving realm. Here's a comprehensive guide to successfully navigate the gig economy and freelancing:

Understanding the Gig Economy:

- **Definition:** The gig economy refers to a labor market characterized by short-term contracts, freelance work, and independent contractors.
- **Diverse Opportunities:** Gigs encompass a wide range of work, from driving for ride-sharing services to offering specialized skills like design, writing, and coding.
- **Flexibility:** Gigs offer the flexibility to choose when and how much you work, making it suitable for those seeking work-life balance.

Freelancing as a Career:

- **Autonomy:** Freelancing empowers you to be your own boss, set your rates, and choose your projects.
- **Varied Clients:** Freelancers work with multiple clients, diversifying their income sources and reducing dependency on a single employer.
- **Challenges:** Inconsistent income, lack of benefits, and self-discipline are challenges freelancers need to manage.

Building a Freelance Business:

- **Niche Focus:** Identify your area of expertise to target specific industries and clients who need your skills.
- **Creating a Portfolio:** Showcase your work through a professional portfolio, demonstrating your capabilities to potential clients.

- **Networking:** Build a network through social media, industry events, and online platforms to connect with potential clients.

Securing Gigs:

- **Freelance Platforms:** Register on freelance websites like Upwork, Freelancer, or Fiverr to access a global client base.
- **Cold Outreach:** Reach out to potential clients directly, highlighting how your skills can address their needs.
- **Referrals:** Satisfied clients can lead to referrals, generating a steady stream of work.

Financial Management:

- **Budgeting:** Due to irregular income, create a budget that accounts for both busy and lean periods.
- **Emergency Fund:** Establish an emergency fund to navigate income fluctuations and unexpected expenses.
- **Tax Planning:** Freelancers are responsible for their taxes. Set aside a portion of each payment for taxes and consider consulting a tax professional.

Work-Life Balance:

- **Time Management:** Set clear work hours and boundaries to prevent overworking or burnout.
- **Self-Care:** Prioritize self-care to maintain physical and mental well-being while managing the demands of freelancing.

Negotiating and Setting Rates:

- **Research:** Research industry standards and average rates for your skillset to ensure your rates are competitive.
- **Value-Based Pricing:** Instead of just charging by the hour, consider the value your service provides to clients when determining rates.

- **Confidence:** Develop negotiation skills to confidently discuss rates and terms with clients.

Managing Client Relationships:

- **Clear Communication:** Establish expectations upfront, including project scope, deadlines, and payment terms.
- **Contracts:** Use written contracts to outline deliverables, timelines, payment terms, and other crucial details.
- **Professionalism:** Maintain professionalism in all interactions to build a positive reputation and foster long-term relationships.

Continuous Learning and Adaptation:

- **Skill Enhancement:** Invest in continuous learning to stay relevant in a rapidly changing job market.
- **Adapting to Trends:** Stay updated with industry trends and evolving client demands to tailor your offerings.

Starting a Side Business: Steps and Considerations

Embarking on a side business journey can be an exciting and rewarding way to generate extra income, explore your entrepreneurial spirit, and work towards financial independence. However, launching a side business requires careful planning, strategic decision-making, and a solid understanding of the key steps and considerations involved. Here's a comprehensive guide to help you navigate the process of starting a side business:

Identify Your Business Idea:

- **Passion and Expertise:** Choose a business idea that aligns with your passions, skills, and expertise. This ensures that you're motivated and equipped to provide value.
- **Market Demand:** Research the market to identify opportunities where your product or service can address existing needs or solve problems.

Market Research:

- **Target Audience:** Define your target audience's demographics, preferences, and pain points. Tailor your offerings to meet their specific needs.
- **Competitor Analysis:** Study your competitors to identify gaps in the market and differentiate your business.

Business Planning:

- **Business Model:** Determine how your business will operate, whether it's product-based, service-based, subscription-based, or a combination.
- **Business Plan:** Develop a detailed business plan outlining your goals, strategies, financial projections, and marketing approach.

Legal and Financial Considerations:

- **Business Structure:** Choose a legal structure that suits your business, such as sole proprietorship, LLC, or corporation. Each structure has different implications for liability and taxation.
- **Permits and Licenses:** Research and obtain any necessary permits or licenses required to operate legally in your jurisdiction.
- **Finances:** Set up a separate business bank account, establish accounting processes, and determine your initial funding sources.

Branding and Marketing:

- **Business Name:** Choose a memorable and relevant business name that resonates with your target audience.
- **Logo and Visual Identity:** Develop a professional logo and visual identity that reflects your brand's personality.
- **Online Presence:** Create a professional website and establish a strong presence on social media platforms relevant to your industry.

Product or Service Development:

- **Prototyping:** If applicable, create prototypes or samples of your products to test functionality and gather feedback.
- **Quality Assurance:** Ensure that the quality of your product or service meets or exceeds customer expectations.

Sales and Distribution:

- **Sales Channels:** Determine the channels through which you'll sell your products or services, such as e-commerce platforms, your website, or in-person events.
- **Shipping and Fulfillment:** If applicable, set up a reliable shipping and fulfillment process to ensure timely delivery to customers.

Customer Acquisition and Retention:

- **Marketing Strategy:** Develop a marketing strategy that includes both online and offline tactics to attract customers.
- **Customer Relationship Management:** Focus on building strong relationships with your customers through excellent customer service and personalized interactions.

Time Management and Work-Life Balance:

- **Schedule:** Establish a realistic work schedule that balances your side business with your full-time job and personal life.
- **Prioritization:** Prioritize tasks based on their urgency and importance to maximize productivity.

Risk Management:

- **Financial Risk:** Set a budget and monitor your business expenses to avoid financial strain.
- **Legal Risk:** Consult legal professionals to ensure compliance with regulations and minimize legal risks.

Scaling and Growth:

- **Monitoring Performance:** Regularly assess your business's performance against your goals and make necessary adjustments.
- **Expansion:** If your side business gains traction, consider scaling by hiring employees, expanding product lines, or entering new markets.

Personal Development and Learning:

- **Continuous Learning:** Stay updated with industry trends, new technologies, and best practices to enhance your business knowledge.
- **Networking:** Attend industry events and connect with other entrepreneurs to gain insights and potential collaborations.

Balancing Commitments:

- **Full-Time Job:** Maintain open communication with your employer about your side business and ensure it doesn't interfere with your job responsibilities.
- **Family and Personal Time:** Allocate time for your family and personal interests to maintain a healthy work-life balance.

Scaling Up: From Side Hustle to Full-Time Entrepreneurship

Transitioning from a side hustle to full-time entrepreneurship is an exhilarating journey that involves careful planning, strategic decision-making, and a deep commitment to realizing your business's potential. As you embark on this path, navigating the complexities of scaling up requires a comprehensive understanding of the steps and considerations involved. Here's a comprehensive guide to help you successfully transition from a side hustle to full-time entrepreneurship:

Evaluate Readiness:

- **Financial Stability:** Assess your personal financial situation to ensure you have a safety net to cover both personal and business expenses during the transition.
- **Business Viability:** Ensure your side hustle demonstrates consistent demand, steady revenue growth, and a clear path to sustainability.

Create a Transition Plan:

- **Clear Milestones:** Set clear milestones and goals for your business that signal when it's appropriate to transition to full-time entrepreneurship.
- **Financial Plan:** Develop a financial plan that outlines how much savings you need to cover living expenses and business operations during the transition phase.

Diversify Income Streams:

- **Multiple Revenue Streams:** Consider diversifying your income sources to reduce reliance on a single revenue stream. This can provide stability during the transition.
- **Monetize Skills:** Explore opportunities to monetize additional skills

or services that complement your core business offering.

Business Infrastructure:

- **Processes and Systems:** Establish efficient processes and systems that can handle increased demand and workload as your business scales.
- **Outsourcing:** Identify tasks that can be outsourced to freelancers or contractors, allowing you to focus on high-impact activities.

Market Expansion:

- **Target Audience:** Define your target audience more precisely and develop strategies to reach a broader customer base.
- **Marketing Efforts:** Implement robust marketing campaigns to increase brand awareness and attract new customers.

Build a Strong Online Presence:

- **Professional Website:** Ensure your website is well-designed, user-friendly, and effectively communicates your brand's value proposition.
- **Content Strategy:** Develop a content strategy that positions you as an industry expert and engages your target audience.

Networking and Partnerships:

- **Industry Connections:** Build relationships with other entrepreneurs, industry leaders, and potential partners to tap into collaborative opportunities.
- **Collaborations:** Explore partnerships, joint ventures, and collaborations that can enhance your business's reach and credibility.

Legal and Administrative Considerations:

- **Business Structure:** Reassess your business structure and legal obligations, considering tax implications, liability, and growth prospects.

- **Licenses and Permits:** Ensure you have the necessary licenses and permits required for full-time business operations.

Financial Planning:

- **Budget and Projections:** Develop a detailed budget and financial projections that account for both business and personal expenses.
- **Emergency Fund:** Maintain a robust emergency fund to cover unexpected business setbacks or personal emergencies.

Healthcare and Benefits:

- **Health Insurance:** Secure health insurance coverage for yourself and any dependents as you transition away from employer-sponsored benefits.
- **Retirement Planning:** Explore retirement savings options, such as opening a solo 401(k) or contributing to an Individual Retirement Account (IRA).

Mindset Shift:

- **Entrepreneurial Mindset:** Embrace an entrepreneurial mindset, which involves taking calculated risks, embracing change, and adapting to challenges.
- **Commitment and Passion:** Full-time entrepreneurship demands dedication and passion for your business's growth and success.

Continuous Learning:

- **Professional Development:** Invest in ongoing learning to stay updated with industry trends, best practices, and emerging technologies.
- **Adaptation:** Be prepared to adapt and pivot your business strategies

based on market feedback and changing circumstances.

Seek Guidance:

- **Mentorship:** Seek guidance from experienced entrepreneurs or mentors who have successfully transitioned from side hustle to full-time entrepreneurship.
- **Professional Advice:** Consult professionals such as accountants, legal experts, and business advisors to ensure a smooth transition.

Risk Management and Financial Planning for Entrepreneurs

Navigating the entrepreneurial landscape requires a robust risk management strategy and careful financial planning to ensure the success and sustainability of your business. As an entrepreneur, you face various uncertainties, and your ability to identify, assess, and mitigate risks can significantly impact your business's trajectory. Here's an in-depth guide to understanding risk management and implementing effective financial planning strategies for entrepreneurs:

Risk Assessment:

- **Identify Risks:** Identify potential risks that could affect your business, such as market volatility, competition, regulatory changes, or economic downturns.
- **Assess Impact:** Evaluate the potential impact of each risk on your business's operations, finances, and overall objectives.
- **Likelihood:** Determine the likelihood of each risk occurring based on historical data, industry trends, and expert insights.

Risk Mitigation Strategies:

- **Diversification:** Diversify your product or service offerings, customer base, and income streams to reduce dependence on a single source.
- **Insurance:** Consider business insurance policies such as general liability, property, and professional liability insurance to mitigate specific risks.
- **Legal Protections:** Secure intellectual property rights, contracts, and agreements to protect your business's assets and interests.
- **Contingency Planning:** Develop contingency plans for potential disruptions, outlining steps to mitigate the impact of unforeseen events.

Financial Planning for Entrepreneurs:

- **Budgeting:** Create a comprehensive budget that outlines your business's income, expenses, and financial goals.
- **Cash Flow Management:** Monitor and manage your cash flow to ensure your business can cover operating expenses and investments.
- **Emergency Fund:** Maintain an emergency fund to cover unexpected expenses or revenue shortfalls.

Forecasting and Projection:

- **Sales Forecasts:** Develop sales projections based on market trends, historical data, and your marketing and sales strategies.
- **Financial Projections:** Prepare financial projections that outline revenue, expenses, and profitability over a specified period.

Investment and Growth:

- **Capital Allocation:** Allocate funds strategically between day-to-day operations and investments for growth.
- **ROI Analysis:** Conduct a return on investment (ROI) analysis for potential business initiatives to assess their financial viability.

Debt Management:

- **Debt Strategy:** If you plan to take on debt, carefully consider the purpose, terms, and repayment plan to ensure it aligns with your business's financial goals.
- **Debt-to-Equity Ratio:** Maintain a healthy balance between debt and equity to avoid excessive financial risk.

Tax Planning:

- **Tax Obligations:** Understand your business's tax obligations, including income tax, sales tax, and self-employment tax.

- **Tax-Efficient Strategies:** Implement tax-efficient strategies to minimize your tax liability while remaining compliant with tax regulations.

Retirement Planning:

- **Personal Retirement:** Establish a retirement savings plan, such as a Simplified Employee Pension (SEP) IRA or a Solo 401(k), to secure your financial future.
- **Business Succession Planning:** Develop a plan for the long-term continuation of your business, whether through passing it on to a successor or selling it.

Stress Testing and Scenario Planning:

- **Scenario Analysis:** Conduct scenario analysis to evaluate how different economic or industry scenarios could impact your business's financial health.
- **Stress Testing:** Assess your business's ability to withstand unexpected challenges by simulating adverse scenarios.

Professional Advice:

- **Consult Experts:** Seek guidance from financial advisors, accountants, and legal professionals who specialize in working with entrepreneurs.
- **Peer Networking:** Connect with fellow entrepreneurs to share insights, experiences, and best practices in risk management and financial planning.

Adaptability and Review:

- **Continuous Review:** Regularly review your risk management and financial planning strategies to ensure they align with changing business circumstances.

- **Adaptability:** Be prepared to adapt your strategies based on market shifts, regulatory changes, and other external factors.

By integrating comprehensive risk management and prudent financial planning, entrepreneurs can fortify their businesses against uncertainties and position themselves for growth and long-term success. Understanding, assessing, and addressing risks while maintaining a disciplined financial approach will contribute to a resilient and thriving entrepreneurial journey.

Understanding Geographic Arbitrage and Its Benefits

Geographic arbitrage is a concept that has gained prominence in the modern world of global connectivity and remote work opportunities. It refers to the practice of leveraging disparities in costs of living, wages, and economic conditions between different geographic locations to enhance one's financial position. By strategically choosing where to live and work, individuals can optimize their income, expenses, and overall quality of life. Here's a comprehensive guide to understanding geographic arbitrage and the benefits it offers:

Defining Geographic Arbitrage:

- **Cost Disparities:** Geographic arbitrage exploits variations in costs of living, housing, services, and other expenses across different regions.
- **Income Opportunities:** It capitalizes on earning potential differences, allowing individuals to earn in a higher-paying location while benefiting from lower expenses elsewhere.

Benefits of Geographic Arbitrage:

- **Enhanced Savings:** By living in a location with a lower cost of living, individuals can save a larger portion of their income.
- **Investment Opportunities:** Increased savings can be directed toward investments, accelerating wealth accumulation and financial independence.
- **Quality of Life:** Geographic arbitrage can lead to an improved standard of living, as individuals can afford better amenities and experiences.
- **Early Retirement:** Leveraging geographic arbitrage may expedite the path to early retirement by optimizing income and expenses.

Factors Influencing Geographic Arbitrage:

- **Wage Disparities:** Different regions offer varying wage levels for similar roles, allowing individuals to earn more in high-wage locations.
- **Housing Costs:** Housing costs can significantly differ between areas, enabling individuals to reduce a substantial expense through strategic relocation.
- **Healthcare and Education:** Locations with affordable healthcare and education options can contribute to cost savings.
- **Taxation:** Tax policies differ across regions, impacting overall financial positioning.

Strategies for Geographic Arbitrage:

- **Remote Work:** The rise of remote work enables individuals to earn a competitive income while living in a location with a lower cost of living.
- **Digital Entrepreneurship:** Online businesses allow individuals to generate income irrespective of their physical location.
- **Retirement Destinations:** Relocating to retirement-friendly regions with lower costs can extend retirement savings.
- **Job Flexibility:** Seeking job opportunities in regions with strong demand for specific skills can lead to higher compensation.

Research and Planning:

- **Cost Analysis:** Research and compare living costs, including housing, transportation, food, and other essentials, across potential locations.
- **Income Evaluation:** Assess income opportunities available in different regions, considering job prospects and industry demand.
- **Quality of Life:** Evaluate the overall quality of life, including healthcare, education, cultural activities, and community, in potential destinations.

Challenges and Considerations:

- **Cultural Adjustment:** Moving to a new location may involve adapting to a different culture, language, and lifestyle.
- **Family and Relationships:** Geographic arbitrage can impact family dynamics, especially if family members have to relocate as well.
- **Long-Term Planning:** Consider the long-term implications of location choices on career progression, family, and financial goals.

Tax and Legal Implications:

- **Residency Rules:** Understand the residency rules and tax implications of your chosen location to optimize your tax strategy.
- **Legal Requirements:** Research visa, immigration, and legal requirements when moving to a new country or region.

Digital Connectivity and Globalization:

- **Technological Advancements:** The proliferation of technology and digital communication tools enables remote work and online businesses.
- **Global Marketplace:** Access to a global market allows entrepreneurs to reach clients and customers worldwide.

Environmental and Lifestyle Considerations:

- **Eco-Friendly Locations:** Choosing locations with a lower carbon footprint and eco-friendly initiatives aligns with sustainability goals.
- **Preferred Lifestyle:** Opt for locations that align with your preferred lifestyle, hobbies, and recreational opportunities.

Geographic arbitrage presents an intriguing opportunity for individuals to optimize their financial situation while enjoying an improved quality of life. By strategically leveraging disparities in income and expenses across different geographic regions, individuals can work towards their financial goals more effectively and potentially accelerate their path to financial independence.

Researching Cost of Living Differences

One of the key factors in effectively leveraging geographic arbitrage is a thorough understanding of the cost of living differences between various geographic locations. Researching these differences empowers individuals to make informed decisions about where to live and work to optimize their financial situation. Here's a comprehensive guide to researching cost of living differences and using this information to your advantage:

Defining Cost of Living:

- **Essential Expenses:** The cost of living encompasses essential expenses such as housing, transportation, groceries, healthcare, utilities, and education.
- **Relative Measurements:** Cost of living is often compared as an index relative to a base location, which is assigned a value of 100. Locations with higher values have a higher cost of living.

Researching Cost of Living:

- **Online Cost of Living Calculators:** Utilize online tools and calculators that provide a detailed breakdown of cost of living differences between cities, regions, and countries.
- **Comparative Websites:** Visit websites that aggregate data from various sources to provide comprehensive cost of living comparisons.
- **Government Data:** Some government agencies publish official data on consumer prices, inflation rates, and other economic indicators.

Components of Cost of Living:

- **Housing:** Investigate average rents, home prices, and property taxes in potential locations.
- **Transportation:** Research costs related to commuting, public transportation, fuel, and vehicle ownership.

- **Groceries and Food:** Compare the prices of common groceries, dining out, and food delivery services.
- **Healthcare:** Research healthcare costs, including insurance premiums, medical services, and prescription medication.
- **Utilities:** Assess expenses for electricity, water, heating, cooling, and internet services.
- **Education:** If applicable, research education costs such as tuition fees and related expenses.

Quality of Life Factors:

- **Cultural Activities:** Research entertainment options, museums, theaters, and other cultural activities in different locations.
- **Recreational Opportunities:** Explore outdoor spaces, parks, recreational facilities, and sports activities.
- **Dining and Cuisine:** Consider the availability and affordability of local dining options and cuisines.
- **Safety and Security:** Research crime rates, safety measures, and community well-being in potential locations.

Currency Exchange Rates:

- **Foreign Exchange:** If considering an international move, research currency exchange rates and their impact on your purchasing power.

Local Insights:

- **Connect with Locals:** Reach out to residents of the target location to gain insights into the local cost of living and lifestyle.
- **Online Forums:** Participate in online forums and expat communities to gather firsthand experiences and advice.

Considerations for Remote Work:

- **Income and Expenses:** Evaluate whether your remote work income aligns with the cost of living in your chosen location.

- **Digital Nomad Communities:** Join digital nomad communities to connect with others who have experience living and working in various locations.

Comparing Multiple Locations:

- **Create a Spreadsheet:** Compile data from different locations in a spreadsheet to compare key expenses and quality of life factors side by side.
- **Weighting Priorities:** Assign weights to various expenses based on their importance to you to arrive at a personalized cost of living index.

Financial Implications:

- **Savings Potential:** Calculate potential savings by subtracting your estimated expenses from your expected income in each location.
- **Investment Opportunities:** Consider how cost of living differences may affect your ability to invest and grow your wealth.

Long-Term Impact:

- **Career Progression:** Assess how the cost of living differences may impact your career growth and opportunities.
- **Family Considerations:** Consider the implications of your decision on your family members and their well-being.

Holistic Evaluation:

- **Balancing Factors:** Evaluate the cost of living alongside other factors such as job opportunities, lifestyle preferences, and personal goals.
- **Trial Period:** Consider spending an extended period in the target location to experience the cost of living firsthand before making a permanent decision.

Researching cost of living differences is a vital step in optimizing your financial situation through geographic arbitrage. By conducting thorough research and considering both financial and lifestyle aspects, you can make an informed choice that aligns with your goals and aspirations, leading to an improved quality of life and enhanced financial well-being.

Evaluating Job Opportunities in Lower Cost Areas

When considering geographic arbitrage, a key aspect is evaluating job opportunities in lower cost areas to maximize your income while benefiting from reduced expenses. Strategic job selection plays a crucial role in achieving financial optimization and a better quality of life. Here's a comprehensive guide to effectively evaluate job opportunities in lower cost areas:

Researching Job Markets:

- **Industry Demand:** Research industries that are thriving in the target area and have a strong demand for your skills.
- **Job Portals:** Explore online job portals and professional networking platforms that list job opportunities in specific regions.
- **Local Companies:** Look into local companies and startups that align with your expertise and career goals.

Salary Research:

- **Local Salary Data:** Gather information about typical salaries for your role in the chosen location.
- **Cost of Living Adjustments:** Consider how potential salaries align with the local cost of living, aiming for higher purchasing power.

Remote Work Opportunities:

- **Remote-Friendly Companies:** Look for companies that offer remote work options, allowing you to work from a lower cost area while earning a competitive salary.
- **Freelance and Consulting:** Explore opportunities for freelancing, consulting, or contracting, which can provide flexibility and income diversity.

Quality of Opportunities:

- **Career Growth:** Evaluate if the job offers opportunities for career advancement, skill development, and professional growth.
- **Industry Relevance:** Consider the relevance of the job to your industry and long-term career goals.

Networking and Connections:

- **Local Networking:** Attend local industry events, workshops, and meetups to connect with professionals in the area.
- **Online Networking:** Engage in online forums, social media groups, and networking platforms to expand your connections.

Remote Work Skills:

- **Tech Proficiency:** Develop strong remote work skills, including effective communication, time management, and the ability to work independently.
- **Virtual Collaboration:** Master tools and software for virtual collaboration, project management, and remote team communication.

Flexibility and Lifestyle:

- **Work-Life Balance:** Evaluate the job's flexibility and potential impact on achieving a desirable work-life balance.
- **Location Independence:** Assess the extent to which the job allows you to work remotely or adopt a flexible work arrangement.

Company Culture:

- **Values and Mission:** Assess the alignment of the company's values and mission with your personal and professional aspirations.
- **Employee Satisfaction:** Research employee reviews and satisfaction

to gauge the work environment and company culture.

Benefits and Perks:

- **Compensation Package:** Evaluate the entire compensation package, including benefits, bonuses, and other perks.
- **Healthcare and Insurance:** Consider healthcare coverage and insurance options provided by the employer.

Long-Term Viability:

- **Industry Trends:** Analyze the industry's growth prospects and long-term viability in the chosen location.
- **Economic Stability:** Research the area's economic stability and potential for sustained job opportunities.

Remote Work Infrastructure:

- **Internet Connectivity:** Ensure the target area has reliable high-speed internet connectivity, a critical factor for remote work.
- **Co-Working Spaces:** Research the availability of co-working spaces or remote work-friendly environments.

Negotiating Compensation:

- **Cost of Living Adjustment:** In negotiations, consider highlighting the cost of living differences to negotiate a competitive salary.
- **Remote Work Value:** Emphasize your ability to contribute remotely and the value you bring to the company.

Transitioning Seamlessly:

- **Trial Period:** Consider testing the arrangement with a short-term stay before committing to a permanent move.
- **Gradual Transition:** Plan a gradual transition to ensure a smooth

adjustment to the new location and work arrangement.

Evaluating job opportunities in lower cost areas requires a strategic approach that considers both financial considerations and your career aspirations. By thoroughly researching the job market, assessing salary data, and evaluating the potential for career growth and lifestyle fit, you can make an informed decision that aligns with your goals and positions you for success in your chosen location.

Challenges and Considerations of Relocating

Relocating to a new area, whether for financial optimization, career opportunities, or lifestyle changes, can be both exciting and challenging. While the benefits of geographic arbitrage and new beginnings are appealing, it's essential to be aware of the potential challenges and considerations that come with the decision to relocate. Here's a comprehensive guide to navigating the challenges and considerations of relocating:

Cultural Adjustment:

- **Cultural Differences:** Prepare for cultural variations in customs, language, traditions, and social norms.
- **Mindset Shift:** Embrace an open mindset to adapt to and appreciate the new culture and ways of living.

Family and Relationships:

- **Family Considerations:** Consider how the move will impact your family members, especially children and their education.
- **Spouse's Career:** Evaluate potential job opportunities and career prospects for your spouse in the new location.

Social Network:

- **Leaving Support Systems:** Relocating may mean leaving behind friends, family, and established social networks.
- **Building New Connections:** Proactively engage in social activities, clubs, and local events to build a new social circle.

Professional Transition:

- **Job Opportunities:** Assess the availability of suitable job opportunities and your ability to transition smoothly.
- **Market Demand:** Research the demand for your skills and industry

in the new location.

Financial Considerations:

- **Cost of Living Changes:** Be prepared for potential adjustments in your budget due to differences in expenses.
- **Income Stability:** Ensure a stable income source in the new location to support your lifestyle.

Logistical Challenges:

- **Moving Logistics:** Plan the logistics of moving, including packing, transportation, and settling in.
- **Legal Requirements:** Research visa, work permits, and legal formalities required for the new location.

Housing and Accommodation:

- **Housing Search:** Research housing options that align with your preferences and budget.
- **Lease Terms:** Review lease agreements and terms to ensure they suit your plans and expectations.

Healthcare Access:

- **Healthcare Facilities:** Research healthcare providers, insurance coverage, and medical facilities in the new area.
- **Medical Records Transfer:** Ensure a smooth transfer of medical records to the new healthcare providers.

Education:

- **School Options:** Research schools for your children, considering their academic needs and extracurricular interests.
- **Education Quality:** Evaluate the quality of education and the

compatibility of the curriculum.

Emotional Well-being:

- **Emotional Challenges:** Be prepared for moments of homesickness and nostalgia, especially during the initial period.
- **Support Systems:** Build a support system of friends, colleagues, and fellow newcomers to share experiences.

Weather and Climate:

- **Climate Adjustment:** Adjust to changes in weather conditions, which can impact daily routines and activities.

Lifestyle Fit:

- **Lifestyle Expectations:** Consider if the new location aligns with your preferred lifestyle, interests, and hobbies.
- **Amenities and Services:** Assess the availability of amenities, recreational facilities, and services.

Language Barrier:

- **Language Skills:** If moving to an area with a different language, consider learning the local language to facilitate communication.

Long-Term Planning:

- **Sustainability:** Evaluate if the new location aligns with your long-term goals, both personally and professionally.
- **Exit Strategy:** Have a plan in place in case you need to relocate again or if the move doesn't meet your expectations.

Resilience and Adaptability:

- **Adaptive Mindset:** Cultivate resilience and adaptability to effectively overcome challenges and adjust to the new environment.

- **Patience:** Understand that adapting to a new location takes time, and challenges are part of the process.

Relocating involves a mix of excitement and challenges. By addressing potential challenges proactively and considering all relevant factors, you can make an informed decision and approach your new adventure with a realistic perspective. Through careful planning, research, and an open mindset, you can navigate the transition successfully and embrace the opportunities that come with relocating.

Managing Remote Work and Building a Portable Career

The rise of remote work has opened up new opportunities for individuals to create portable careers that allow them to work from anywhere in the world. Whether you're seeking geographic arbitrage, a flexible lifestyle, or the ability to travel while earning an income, building a portable career requires effective management and strategic planning. Here's a comprehensive guide to managing remote work and crafting a successful portable career:

Defining a Portable Career:

- **Location Independence:** A portable career allows you to work from various locations, giving you the flexibility to adapt to changing circumstances.
- **Diverse Income Streams:** Building multiple income streams that can be managed remotely is a hallmark of a portable career.

Choosing the Right Path:

- **Skills Assessment:** Identify your strengths, skills, and expertise that can be leveraged in a remote work setting.
- **Remote-Friendly Industries:** Research industries and roles that offer remote work opportunities aligned with your skills.

Building a Skill Set:

- **Remote Work Skills:** Develop skills such as effective communication, time management, self-discipline, and proficiency with remote collaboration tools.
- **Digital Literacy:** Master technology tools that facilitate remote work, such as project management software and virtual communication platforms.

Remote Work Strategies:

- **Flexible Work Schedule:** Establish a work routine that suits your productivity peaks while accommodating time zone differences if applicable.
- **Designated Workspace:** Create a dedicated workspace that promotes focus and separates work from personal life.
- **Communication:** Maintain clear and regular communication with colleagues, clients, and collaborators to ensure effective collaboration.

Building a Portable Career:

- **Freelancing and Consulting:** Offer your skills and expertise as a freelancer or consultant to clients across the globe.
- **Online Business:** Create an online business, such as e-commerce, content creation, or online courses, that generates income regardless of your location.
- **Remote Jobs:** Seek out remote job opportunities with companies that support a flexible work arrangement.

Creating a Brand:

- **Personal Branding:** Build a strong online presence through social media, a professional website, and a well-crafted online portfolio.
- **Showcase Expertise:** Share your knowledge through blogging, podcasts, webinars, or public speaking to establish authority in your field.

Income Diversification:

- **Multiple Revenue Streams:** Explore different income streams within your portable career, such as consulting, teaching, writing, or affiliate marketing.
- **Passive Income:** Invest in creating products, content, or assets that generate passive income over time.

Financial Management:

- **Budgeting:** Set up a budget that considers your variable income and potential currency fluctuations when working internationally.
- **Emergency Fund:** Maintain a robust emergency fund to handle unexpected expenses or fluctuations in income.

Networking and Collaboration:

- **Online Communities:** Join remote work and digital nomad communities to connect with like-minded professionals, share insights, and find potential collaborators.
- **Collaborative Projects:** Partner with others on projects that capitalize on your combined skills and expertise.

Continuous Learning:

- **Skill Enhancement:** Stay updated on industry trends and advancements by engaging in continuous learning and professional development.
- **Adaptability:** Be open to learning new skills and adapting to changes in your field to remain relevant.

Work-Life Balance:

- **Boundaries:** Set clear boundaries between work and personal life to prevent burnout and maintain a healthy work-life balance.
- **Wellness:** Prioritize self-care, exercise, and mindfulness practices to enhance your overall well-being.

Legal and Tax Considerations:

- **Legal Structure:** Depending on your career path, consider the legal structure that best suits your business, such as freelancing, sole proprietorship, LLC, or corporation.

- **Tax Implications:** Research tax regulations in your home country and the countries you operate in to ensure compliance.

Crafting a successful portable career requires careful planning, dedication, and adaptability. By honing your remote work skills, building a strong online presence, diversifying your income streams, and embracing a flexible mindset, you can create a fulfilling and sustainable career that provides both financial freedom and the freedom to work from anywhere you choose.

Developing a Financial Independence Mindset

Achieving financial independence is not only about following specific strategies and techniques; it's also about cultivating the right mindset that aligns with your goals and empowers you to make effective financial decisions. A financial independence mindset involves adopting attitudes and beliefs that support your journey towards financial freedom. Here's a comprehensive guide to developing a financial independence mindset:

Clarity of Goals:

- **Defining Priorities:** Clearly define your financial goals, both short-term and long-term, to give your efforts purpose and direction.
- **Visualization:** Visualize your ideal financial future to motivate and inspire yourself to take consistent action.

Positive Beliefs:

- **Belief in Possibility:** Believe that achieving financial independence is attainable through determination, education, and disciplined efforts.
- **Self-Worth:** Recognize your own value and potential to create financial success.

Financial Responsibility:

- **Ownership:** Take full ownership of your financial decisions and outcomes, avoiding blame or excuses.
- **Accountability:** Hold yourself accountable for managing your finances and making informed choices.

Mindful Spending:

- **Intentional Choices:** Make spending decisions consciously,

considering the alignment with your goals and the value the purchase adds to your life.
- **Delayed Gratification:** Practice delaying non-essential purchases to focus on your long-term financial well-being.

Debt Management:

- **Debt-Free Mindset:** Cultivate a mindset that seeks to reduce and eliminate debt to free yourself from financial burdens.
- **Responsible Borrowing:** If borrowing is necessary, do so strategically and responsibly, considering the impact on your financial goals.

Savings and Investment Focus:

- **Pay Yourself First:** Prioritize saving and investing by treating them as non-negotiable expenses.
- **Long-Term View:** Embrace a long-term perspective when it comes to saving and investing, understanding the power of compounding.

Risk-Taking and Learning:

- **Calculated Risks:** Be open to calculated risks that align with your goals, whether in investments or entrepreneurial endeavors.
- **Continuous Learning:** Recognize that knowledge is a valuable asset; invest in your financial education to make informed decisions.

Resilience and Persistence:

- **Adaptability:** Embrace change and adapt to unexpected challenges, knowing that setbacks are opportunities for growth.
- **Persistent Effort:** Commit to consistency and determination, understanding that achieving financial independence requires time and effort.

Contentment and Gratitude:

- **Appreciation:** Cultivate gratitude for what you have rather than constantly striving for more.
- **Contentment:** Find contentment in experiences, relationships, and personal growth, reducing the need for excessive material possessions.

Delayed Gratification:

- **Patience:** Develop patience and the ability to wait for rewards, recognizing that instant gratification can hinder long-term financial progress.
- **Future-Oriented:** Prioritize future financial well-being over immediate desires.

Overcoming Financial Fears:

- **Fear Management:** Identify and address financial fears, such as fear of failure or fear of missing out, to prevent them from dictating your decisions.
- **Empowerment:** Replace fear with knowledge and action to gain control over your financial situation.

Community and Support:

- **Surrounding Influence:** Surround yourself with individuals who share similar financial values and goals.
- **Support Networks:** Join financial forums, attend seminars, and engage in discussions to gain insights and motivation from others.

Self-Care and Well-being:

- **Balanced Lifestyle:** Prioritize your well-being by maintaining a balanced lifestyle that promotes physical, emotional, and mental health.

- **Stress Management:** Develop healthy coping mechanisms to manage financial stress and anxiety effectively.

Giving Back:

- **Generosity:** Incorporate a spirit of giving into your financial journey by supporting causes and organizations aligned with your values.
- **Abundance Mindset:** Cultivate an abundance mindset by acknowledging your ability to contribute positively to others' lives.

Developing a financial independence mindset is a journey that involves reshaping your beliefs, behaviors, and attitudes towards money. By focusing on positivity, responsibility, continuous learning, and aligning your actions with your financial goals, you can foster a mindset that propels you towards achieving financial independence and creating a more fulfilling and purposeful life.

Overcoming Common Psychological Barriers

As you embark on your journey towards financial independence, you may encounter various psychological barriers that can impede your progress and decision-making. These barriers are often rooted in emotions, fears, and limiting beliefs that can hinder your ability to take effective actions. Overcoming these psychological barriers is essential to creating a clear path towards your financial goals. Here's a comprehensive guide to identifying and overcoming common psychological barriers:

Fear of Failure:

- **Shifting Perspective:** Reframe failure as a valuable learning experience that brings you closer to your goals.
- **Small Steps:** Break down your financial goals into smaller, manageable steps to reduce the fear of overwhelming failure.

Fear of Change:

- **Embrace Uncertainty:** Recognize that change is inevitable and often leads to growth and new opportunities.
- **Focus on Benefits:** List the potential positive outcomes of change, such as increased financial security and personal growth.

Procrastination:

- **Setting Deadlines:** Establish clear deadlines for financial tasks to create a sense of urgency.
- **Start Small:** Begin with small, manageable tasks to build momentum and overcome the inertia of procrastination.

Impulse Spending:

- **Mindful Consumption:** Pause and reflect on purchases, considering whether they align with your financial goals and values.

- **Delay Gratification:** Implement a 24-hour rule before making non-essential purchases to prevent impulsive buying.

Negative Self-Talk:

- **Positive Affirmations:** Replace negative thoughts with positive affirmations that reinforce your ability to achieve financial success.
- **Self-Compassion:** Practice self-compassion by treating yourself kindly and forgiving past financial mistakes.

Comparison Trap:

- **Focus on Progress:** Measure your success against your own progress rather than comparing yourself to others.
- **Celebrate Milestones:** Celebrate your achievements, no matter how small, to boost your self-esteem and motivation.

Sunk Cost Fallacy:

- **Future-Oriented Decision Making:** Base decisions on future potential rather than past investments that cannot be recovered.
- **Cutting Losses:** Recognize when to let go of unproductive financial ventures, even if you've invested time or resources.

Lack of Self-Worth:

- **Recognize Value:** Acknowledge your skills, abilities, and potential to achieve financial success.
- **Seek Support:** Surround yourself with individuals who believe in your abilities and encourage your growth.

Overcoming Loss Aversion:

- **Rational Assessment:** Make decisions based on logical analysis rather than being driven solely by the fear of losses.

- **Long-Term Perspective:** Consider the long-term benefits of financial decisions, focusing on the potential gains.

Delaying Financial Planning:

- **Start Today:** Understand that the sooner you start, the more time you have to leverage compounding and reach your goals.
- **Small Steps:** Begin with simple financial actions, such as creating a budget or setting up an emergency fund.

Perfectionism:

- **Embrace Imperfection:** Accept that mistakes are a natural part of the learning process and allow yourself room for growth.
- **Progress Over Perfection:** Prioritize progress towards your goals over seeking perfection in every financial decision.

Overcoming psychological barriers requires self-awareness, commitment, and a willingness to challenge your beliefs and behaviors. By adopting strategies that shift your mindset, build resilience, and promote positive financial habits, you can overcome these barriers and navigate your journey towards financial independence with confidence and clarity. Remember that every step forward, no matter how small, brings you closer to your goals.

Balancing Delayed Gratification with Present Enjoyment

Striking a balance between delayed gratification and present enjoyment is a fundamental aspect of the journey towards financial independence. While delaying certain pleasures can lead to long-term financial success, it's equally important to find joy and fulfillment in the present moment. Achieving this balance requires mindful decision-making and a holistic approach to your financial and personal well-being. Here's a comprehensive guide to balancing delayed gratification with present enjoyment:

Understanding Delayed Gratification:

- **Long-Term Benefits:** Recognize that delaying immediate pleasures can lead to greater rewards and financial security in the future.
- **Sacrifice for Goals:** Embrace the notion that short-term sacrifices can pave the way for achieving meaningful financial goals.

Setting Financial Goals:

- **Clear Objectives:** Define specific financial goals that inspire you to commit to delayed gratification.
- **Visualization:** Envision the benefits of achieving your goals to reinforce your commitment to long-term planning.

Prioritizing Essentials:

- **Basic Needs:** Ensure your essential needs are met before allocating funds to discretionary spending.
- **Emergency Fund:** Build a robust emergency fund to provide a safety net during unexpected events.

Mindful Spending:

- **Value-Based Spending:** Align spending with your values and

priorities, focusing on experiences that bring lasting joy.
- **Non-Essential Splurges:** Set aside a portion of your budget for occasional indulgences without compromising long-term goals.

Creating Milestones:

- **Celebrate Progress:** Set milestones and celebrate your achievements along the way to financial independence.
- **Reward System:** Establish a reward system that acknowledges your efforts and achievements, reinforcing the value of delayed gratification.

Mindful Present Enjoyment:

- **Mindfulness Practices:** Engage in mindfulness techniques to fully experience and appreciate the present moment.
- **Quality Experiences:** Seek enriching experiences that bring joy and contribute to your well-being.

Flexible Budgeting:

- **Allocating for Fun:** Incorporate a category in your budget specifically for leisure activities and present enjoyment.
- **Percentage Approach:** Allocate a percentage of your income towards both long-term goals and present enjoyment.

Experiences Over Possessions:

- **Collect Memories:** Prioritize experiences, adventures, and memories over accumulating material possessions.
- **Minimalism:** Embrace minimalism to focus on what truly matters and reduce the allure of excessive consumerism.

Savoring Moments:

- **Gratitude Practice:** Cultivate gratitude for the present moments and experiences that enhance your quality of life.
- **Positive Reflection:** Reflect on positive experiences and accomplishments to reinforce a sense of fulfillment.

Balancing Trade-Offs:

- **Opportunity Cost:** Understand the trade-offs associated with immediate indulgences and their potential impact on long-term goals.
- **Conscious Choices:** Make intentional choices by evaluating the trade-offs between present enjoyment and delayed gratification.

Self-Care and Well-being:

- **Holistic Approach:** Recognize that financial well-being is interconnected with physical, emotional, and mental well-being.
- **Invest in Health:** Allocate resources to activities that promote your overall health and well-being.

Open Communication:

- **Shared Values:** Discuss financial goals and the balance between present enjoyment and delayed gratification with your family or partner.
- **Collaborative Decisions:** Involve loved ones in financial decisions to ensure a shared understanding of priorities.

Continuous Assessment:

- **Regular Review:** Periodically evaluate your financial goals and lifestyle choices to ensure they align with your evolving values.
- **Adjustments:** Be open to making adjustments to your approach as circumstances and priorities change.

Balancing delayed gratification with present enjoyment is a skill that evolves over time. By combining the benefits of disciplined financial planning with the joy of living in the moment, you can create a fulfilling and well-rounded life that encompasses both short-term pleasures and long-term security. Remember that achieving financial independence is not about sacrificing happiness today for the promise of tomorrow; it's about finding harmony between the two to create a life of purpose and abundance.

The Role of Mindfulness and Stress Management

On the journey to financial independence, the demands of budgeting, investing, and planning can create stress and overwhelm. Mindfulness and effective stress management techniques play a pivotal role in maintaining your emotional well-being, enhancing decision-making, and promoting a balanced approach to achieving your financial goals. Here's a comprehensive guide to understanding the role of mindfulness and stress management in your pursuit of financial independence:

Mindfulness for Financial Well-being:

- **Present-Moment Awareness:** Practice mindfulness to stay present, reducing anxiety about the future or regrets about the past.
- **Reduced Impulsive Decisions:** Mindfulness helps you pause and consider decisions more thoughtfully, preventing impulsive actions.

Stress Management Strategies:

- **Deep Breathing:** Use deep breathing exercises to calm the nervous system and alleviate stress during challenging financial situations.
- **Physical Activity:** Engage in regular physical activity to release endorphins and reduce stress hormones.
- **Mind-Body Practices:** Incorporate yoga, meditation, or tai chi into your routine to promote relaxation and mental clarity.

Financial Stress Awareness:

- **Identify Triggers:** Recognize financial stress triggers, such as debt or market fluctuations, to proactively address them.
- **Open Dialogue:** Share financial concerns with trusted friends, family, or a financial advisor to gain support and perspective.

Cultivating Resilience:

- **Positive Outlook:** Cultivate optimism to view challenges as opportunities for growth rather than insurmountable obstacles.
- **Adaptability:** Develop the ability to adapt to changes and setbacks, maintaining focus on long-term goals.

Mindful Decision-Making:

- **Thoughtful Reflection:** Mindfulness fosters a clear state of mind, enabling you to make financial decisions based on rational analysis.
- **Detached Perspective:** Observe your thoughts and emotions related to finances without being overwhelmed by them.

Work-Life Balance:

- **Set Boundaries:** Establish clear boundaries between work and personal time to prevent burnout.
- **Scheduled Breaks:** Incorporate regular breaks throughout the day to recharge and maintain productivity.

Financial Planning Mindfulness:

- **Focused Attention:** Practice mindful financial planning by giving your full attention to each aspect of your budget and investments.
- **Reduced Anxiety:** Mindfulness reduces anxiety about the unknown by focusing on the information and tools available to you.

Stress-Reducing Habits:

- **Journaling:** Write down your financial worries, emotions, and progress to gain clarity and release tension.
- **Gratitude Practice:** Cultivate gratitude by focusing on the positive aspects of your financial journey, no matter how small.

Mindful Consumption:

- **Conscious Spending:** Apply mindfulness to spending decisions, evaluating whether purchases align with your values and goals.
- **Delayed Gratification:** Choose delayed gratification mindfully, understanding its benefits for long-term financial well-being.

Time Management:

- **Prioritization:** Use mindful prioritization to allocate time to both financial tasks and leisure activities.
- **One Task at a Time:** Engage fully in one task before moving on to the next, promoting efficiency and reducing stress.

Self-Compassion:

- **Non-Judgment:** Be kind to yourself when facing financial challenges or setbacks, understanding that mistakes are part of the journey.
- **Inner Encouragement:** Offer yourself words of encouragement and support in the face of financial stress.

Regular Self-Care:

- **Wellness Routine:** Design a self-care routine that includes activities promoting physical, emotional, and mental well-being.
- **Consistency:** Prioritize self-care consistently to build resilience against financial stressors.

Mindfulness and stress management are essential tools for maintaining emotional equilibrium and making clear-headed financial decisions. By integrating these practices into your daily life, you can navigate the challenges of the financial journey with greater calm, focus, and balance. Remember that achieving financial independence is a holistic pursuit that encompasses both financial success and personal well-being.

Celebrating Milestones and Achievements Along the Journey

Reaching milestones and achieving your financial goals is a remarkable accomplishment that deserves recognition and celebration. Celebrating these successes not only provides a sense of accomplishment but also reinforces your commitment to your financial journey. Here's a final guide to embracing the practice of celebrating milestones and achievements throughout your pursuit of financial independence:

Reflecting on Progress:

- **Gratitude:** Take time to express gratitude for the progress you've made and the lessons you've learned.
- **Personal Growth:** Acknowledge the personal growth and development that has come from your financial journey.

Setting Meaningful Milestones:

- **Specific Goals:** Break down larger goals into smaller, manageable milestones that mark your progress.
- **Tangible Achievements:** Define milestones that have tangible outcomes, such as reaching a certain savings threshold or paying off a specific debt.

Private Reflection:

- **Journaling:** Write in a journal to reflect on your journey, your achievements, and the emotions you've experienced.
- **Self-Appreciation:** Acknowledge your determination and dedication, reminding yourself of your capabilities.

Public Celebrations:

- **Share with Loved Ones:** Celebrate with friends and family who

support and encourage you throughout your financial journey.
- **Social Media:** Share your achievements on social media to inspire others and receive positive reinforcement.

Rewarding Yourself:

- **Personal Treat:** Treat yourself to a reward that aligns with your values and goals, such as a meaningful experience or a small indulgence.
- **Symbolic Tokens:** Consider acquiring a symbolic token or item that represents your achievements.

Expressing Self-Compassion:

- **Avoid Comparison:** Celebrate your achievements without comparing them to others'.
- **Self-Love:** Use celebrations as an opportunity to practice self-love and self-compassion.

Reflecting on Challenges:

- **Overcoming Obstacles:** Recognize and celebrate your ability to overcome challenges and setbacks.
- **Resilience:** Highlight the resilience you've developed through your financial journey.

Motivation for the Future:

- **Inspiration:** Use celebrations as a source of inspiration to continue progressing toward your remaining goals.
- **Renewed Energy:** Celebrations can rejuvenate your motivation and remind you of the purpose behind your efforts.

Sharing the Journey:

- **Teaching Opportunity:** Share your journey with others to inspire and educate them about the principles of financial independence.
- **Networking:** Connect with fellow financial independence enthusiasts to celebrate together and learn from each other.

Long-Term Reflection:

- **Legacy Building:** Document your journey and achievements to create a lasting record for future generations.
- **Inspiring Others:** Your story can serve as a source of inspiration for individuals on their own financial paths.

Continued Progress:

- **Sustaining Momentum:** Use celebrations as stepping stones to maintain momentum and drive toward future milestones.
- **Adapting Goals:** Allow celebrations to be a time to reevaluate and adjust your goals as your circumstances evolve.

As you conclude this book and embark on your financial independence journey, remember that every step forward is a victory worth celebrating. By acknowledging your achievements, no matter how small, you reinforce your commitment to your financial goals and cultivate a sense of empowerment. Embrace each milestone as a testament to your dedication and resilience, and use the positive energy generated by celebrations to fuel your continued progress toward a life of financial freedom and fulfillment. Congratulations on taking this transformative journey!

Dear Valued Reader,

As you reach the final pages of "Financial Independence," we sincerely hope that the journey you've embarked upon has been both enlightening and transformative. Just as this book was crafted to guide you on your path to financial freedom, we humbly ask for your assistance in guiding others who seek similar empowerment.

Your honest review can be a beacon of light for fellow readers who are contemplating their own journey toward financial independence. Your insights can help them make informed decisions, find inspiration, and embrace the strategies that resonate most with them.

Whether you found a particular chapter to be exceptionally enlightening, a strategy to be particularly effective, or an aspect of the book that deeply resonated with your personal experience, your thoughts can make a significant impact.

By taking a few moments to share your thoughts, you contribute to a community of individuals working towards a common goal—financial well-being and independence. Your review has the potential to influence and uplift others who are seeking guidance and support on their own paths.

Please consider leaving a review on platforms like Amazon, Goodreads, or other platforms where you obtained your copy of the book. Your words are not just a simple review; they are a powerful testament to the impact of knowledge and the potential for positive change.

We thank you for your time, your dedication to your own journey, and your willingness to help others find their way.

With heartfelt gratitude,

Alex Thompson

Don't miss out!

Visit the website below and you can sign up to receive emails whenever Alex Thompson publishes a new book. There's no charge and no obligation.

https://books2read.com/r/B-A-FEPY-RJMNC

BOOKS 2 READ

Connecting independent readers to independent writers.

Also by Alex Thompson

Alex on Finance

Financial Freedom Roadmap - Achieving Early Retirement through the FIRE Movement

The Art of Strategic Innovation

Beyond Cash - The Evolution of Digital Payment Systems and the Future of Money

Preserving Wealth in Inflationary Times - Strategies for Protecting Your Financial Future

Standalone

Side Hustle Success: Unlocking Your Entrepreneurial Potential

Side Hustle Success: The Ultimate Guide to Passive and Financial Freedom

Mastering the Markets: Advanced Trading Strategies for Success and Ethical Trading Practices

Financial Fortitude

Mastering the Art of Upselling

The Financial Bullet Blueprint

Investing Demystified: A Beginner's Guide to Building Wealth in the Stock Market

Real Estate Riches: Building Wealth through Property Investment

How To Succeed as a Freelancer

Navigating Complex Waters: Advanced Strategies in Portfolio Management

Behavioral Finance and Investor Psychology

Leading with Empathy: Harnessing Emotional Intelligence for Effective Leadership
Financial Independence

www.ingramcontent.com/pod-product-compliance
Lightning Source LLC
LaVergne TN
LVHW052321200926
848481LV00002B/635
* 9 7 9 8 2 2 3 5 4 6 7 9 5 *